# THINKIN
# BIG

# THINKIN BIG

## THE STORY OF JAMES "QUICK" TILLIS
## THE FIGHTIN COWBOY

# QUICK TILLIS

### as told to J. ENGLEMAN PRICE

ECW PRESS

CANADIAN CATALOGUING IN PUBLICATION DATA

Tillis, James, 1957–
Thinkin big: the story of James "Quick" Tillis, the fightin cowboy

ISBN 1-55022-430-1

I. Tillis, James, 1957–    . 2. Boxers (Sports) – United States – Biography.
I. Price, J. Engleman, 1956–    . II. Title.

GVII32.T54A3 2000        796.83'.092        C00-931710-4

Cover and text design by Tania Craan
Back cover photo by Diane Beals
Layout by Mary Bowness
Printed by AGMV

Distributed in Canada by General Distribution Services,
325 Humber Blvd., Toronto, Ontario M9W 7C3
Distributed in the United States by LPC GROUP,
1436 West Randolph Street, Chicago, Illinois, U.S.A. 60607

Published by ECW PRESS
2120 Queen Street East, Suite 200,
Toronto, Ontario, M4E IE2
ecwpress.com

The publication of *Thinkin Big* has been generously
supported by the Government of Canada through the Book Publishing
Industry Development Program.

Canadä

PRINTED AND BOUND IN CANADA

To my sweet little mother, Rose Marie Tillis, a true soldier in God's army.

— James Quick Tillis

"Neither death, nor life . . . nor things present, nor things to come . . . shall be able to separate us from the love of God, which is in Christ Jesus our Lord." May our words do justice to who you were, Mrs. Tillis.

— J. Engleman Price

# TABLE OF CONTENTS

## ACKNOWLEDGEMENTS

You ever been asked to write down all the folks who've helped you? Hey, that's the story of my life, people helpin me, me helpin them. That's the way it oughta be, but I like to mention them still.

First I gotta thank God the Father, the Son, and the Holy Ghost. Three in One — they've always been there for me. I wanna thank my sweet little mother, Rose Marie Tillis, for believin in me and bein my hero. Even though my father, James T. Tillis, Sr., dropped us like a bad habit, I wanna thank him for his athletic ability. Thank you, Rev. Samuel Thomas Fulbright, my stepfather, for gettin us outta bondage.

I'd like to thank all these people for helpin me when I was a kid, little in body, big in dreams: Rev. Lawrence Lakey and Bishop Lewis, who inspired me; Dave Nash, Jessie Thompson, and Hamp Buggs, my football coaches; Mr. Benjamin and Ted Brown, my Red Shield Boys Club managers; Sherman Wild and Edward Duncan, my boxing coaches; Mrs. Alford, my teacher at Dunbar Elementary; Uncle Paul Reed, who taught me how to be tough; Uncle Cortez Nelson, my good friend; Joe Gibson, "Pops," who I love like a dad but wouldn't know me now cuz of his Alzheimer's; Danny Ogans; Dale Bell; Arther Panell; First Baptist Mohawk Church; Lewis Payne, my brother-in-law, who took me to amateur fights.

I'd like to thank all these people for gettin me to the top in boxing. They helped make it happen — Muhammad Ali, my idol; Sugar Ray Robinson, the greatest pound for pound; Keith Beaver Reed, my cousin who taught me those words "jab" and "hook" and got me started; Archie Moore, the old mongoose, my trainer; Whit Lowery and Spider Webb, my trainers; Lenita Tillis, my fifth wife, attorney, manager, and friend; Denna Johnson, a very good companion who helped me so very much; Marvin Jones, my good friend who I love like a dad; Gail Barnes; Attorney Robert Stubbelfield, who got me outta jail; Attorney Jeffrey D. (for Dependable) Jacobs; Jim Kaulentis, thanks for gettin me to the top, I love ya like a father; Dean Kaulentis, his brother, who I love like a dad too; Mark Milstein, Billy Learch, and Bob Alpert, my backers, who I love like brothers; Rory O'Shea, trainer; Joe Kahn, my right hand man; George Seals, my partner; Larry Johnson, my pal; Jack Anque; Walter Tyler; Jack Murphy, my manager; Chris Laveva; Abe Hurschler, who's dead now, God rest his soul; Kenny Lucas; Ankie Lowrey; Harry Wilson, "The World's Oldest Teenager," my pal; Johnny Lira, my trainer; DeDe Armour, my trainer; Melanie Hughes Morris, my first and third wife and good friend; Earl's Health Foods, when my body was so tired; Bundini Brown, trainer and motivator; Gary and Bill Bentley; Van Eden; Ernie Terrell, Don King, Bob Arum, and Cedrick Kushner, promoters and pals; Robert and Janis Hudson, for takin me to Chicago; Lloyd Womack; Herbert Gray; Ronnie Warrior, trainer and friend, who tried to warn me of all the dirt; Nelson Jackson Sr., trainer, and his son, Jackie Jackson; Henry Watson; Judge B.R. Beasley; Steve Collison; Bill Slaton, trainer; and Grady Exber at the Las Vegas Club for sponsoring me.

Thanks to these people who wrote about me and believed I could do it: Jerry Webber, Scott Cherry, Chris Lincoln, Mike Sowell, the *Oklahoma Eagle*, the *Tulsa Tribune*, and the *Tulsa World*.

I thank Alana Wilcox, our editor, for working with us and

having confidence in the story. I like her so much I don't know if I want to fight her 15 rounds or hug her. I thank Jack David, our publisher, for also having faith in the story. If anybody tries to bother you, just tell them this: "If you ever mess with me again, I'm gonna tell my Quick Tillis FRIEND."

Thanks to these friends who got me in the movies and entertained me: Quincy Jones, my pal; Steven Spielberg, my good friend; Kathleen Kennedy and Frank Marshall, producers of *The Color Purple* and good friends; Jimmy Lynch, Mom's Mabley, Leroy and Skillet, Lawanda Page, and Rudy Ray Moore, comedians.

Thanks to my cowboy buddies: Ronnie and Donnie Stevens, Bob Foster, Nelson Jackson Jr., and Ayatullah Muhammad, who love horses and rodeo just like me.

Thanks to those people who've been helpin me since I got back to Tulsa where I belong: Larry and Laura Beasley who helped me out a lot; O'Riley's Parts store on Brookside, for givin me spark plugs for Christmas; Wilson's Barbeque; Attorney Otis Williams; McDonald's store on South Peoria; and KFC on North Lewis, for lettin me and my writer meet every week there even if we didn't eat nothin.

— James Quick Tillis

Thank you, Roger, and my sweet little Lauren for allowing me time to work on a dream I never knew could come true. Thank you, Quick, for seeking me out. Thank you, friends and family, who kept asking, "How's the book coming?" You remembered and it happened.

— J. Engleman Price

# The Woman Named Rose

*Whispering winds sweep past me but I still can't hear a thing.*
*Love of all has passed me by, but my heart still strongly sings.*
*Creative memories come back to me and it was on the tip of my nose*
*that I use those memories to make me feel better*
*As I remembered a woman named Rose.*

*Joy of life can't be found if a loved one's been taken away*
*But you've got to move on and look to be strong*
*To be somebody, someday.*
*The woman I knew was strong in life and always had God on her*
*side*
*And every time I've seen her smile,*
*I light up with pride.*

*Now she's fallen in bad times and been down too,*
*But she picked herself up to see*
*Just how special she knows she is and how loving she could be.*

*Now Rose, it's been so hard thinking of yesterday*
*And I've drowned myself in tears since you took your love away.*
*No one has done the things you done*
*And do things that you do*
*That's why I tried so hard to give all my love to you.*

*Now saddened times fill my lonely days*
*And the roses are gone and the pedals faded away.*
*Only faded memories of our love in my veins exist*
*Times are hard, without your comforting kiss.*

*If only I knew how I can have you back*
*Cause how you left it felt so wrong.*
*Now the times when me and all your children need you the most*
*The time —why, you're gone.*

*Whatever it is, you not here anymore*
*And I know I sit and just cry.*
*Maybe we all should of loved you more*
*Could that be the reason why?*

*Well, I've written this poem and not a song*
*Just to say I'm glad you moved on.*
*Now in heaven you'll wait with God by your side*
*To watch over us to be strong.*

*Not caring about a song or a poem or whatever I chose.*
*When all is said and all is through,*
*In all my tears I'll remember—*
*The woman named Rose.*

—Jamie Tillis Beard (10 years old)
for Grandmother Rose
Written on Mother's Day, 1997

# CHAPTER 1

# THE NIGHT IT ALL STARTED

The fat red and brown roaches crawled between the bars of my cell that month, beggin for some of the stale Rainbow bread I'd have at dinner. I was tryin to get that sick pee smell outta my nose. *Could be worse.* I looked around. Black dudes, white dudes, Mexican dudes, some in for murderin their wives, some for stealin $400 from QuikTrip for a day of crack.

*A bunch of losers and quitters, just hopin to get out one day, maybe even get a real job with benefits and stuff, get a house with a backyard instead of lookin out of some run-down apartment with concrete and yellow lines for a yard. Yeah, they'd get out, all right, but without that needle or bottle or gun, they'd be right back in, back in the can with me.*

They'd taken my teeth. I couldn't even smile at nothin. *I DON'T BELONG HERE. Get me outta this orange suit, don't make me walk outside like some crazy animal with cuffs around my legs and wrists. I'm not like the rest of these losers. I'm not a quitter.*

Sure, who'd believe me? I'd made a quarter million in a few years fightin the best. I'd made the champions wish they'd put someone else in the corner. I'd had my name printed on flashy handbags and jackets, on the Bronco that I paid for in cash. I'd been all over the world, been in the movies, ate dinner with

MOOOvie stars. Never drank, never smoked, never did drugs. Yeah, I was different. I was rottin in a Tulsa jail cell for sendin my $100-a-month child-support checks to the wrong address; I was sendin 'em, she was never gettin 'em. So the judge told me, "get your ass in that six-by-six cell," where I sat writin my story, gettin my pencils sharpened a few times a day by guys wantin to help out a heavyweight contender.

It had all started 33 years ago, one night in 1964 . . .

The old black and white sat where it always sat, on that damn linoleum floor. Kids with snotty noses gobbled down Mama's greasy collard greens and stale cornbread, some aunts and uncles argued about who was gonna watch what. Then Mama took off her apron and looked for an empty spot on the couch — a hard thing to do with seven children. The Tillis family waited for the magic to begin.

"And now, LAAAAdies and gentleman, the two contenders of the evening. The infamous Sonny Liston, HEAAAAAvy-weight CHAMpion of the world. In the other corner, CAAAAASSSSSSIUS CLAAAAY."

The Miami men with them suntans on their faces and their fat, smelly cigars screamed from the TV audience, "KILL HIM, Sonny. Make 'im feel it!"

The proud champion moved around in his corner like he owned the world, shadowboxin the air like he'd already won or somethin.

Clay, the young 22-year-old kid, also shadowboxed in his own corner, but this kid was dancin. A heavyweight dancin on air? No way.

Cassius Clay. I'd heard about this boxer and seen some pictures of him in *Sports Illustrated* at school. But I'd never seen him on television. When I watched him makin moves with his feet like some nervous kid at his first school dance, I had this weird feelin. Somethin was about to happen, I just didn't know what. I could feel it in my blood, real warm like, like it was me doin the fightin.

But I was just a seven-year-old kid, who went to school most days, except when I fooled Mama by fakin a cough or pretendin to have a stomachache. Couldn't fake out Mama too much, though. She knew her two sons and five daughters better than anybody's business, like a mother hen knows every one of her chicks. You couldn't fool Mama.

If I wasn't tryin to skip school, I was out chasin the neighbor girls or stealin other boys' bicycle parts, like the handlebars or the padded seats. I was a bad little boy. I used to walk right up to some eight-year-old boy who was bigger than me, hit him in the face with my scrawny, dirty fist, and then run like hell, hidin behind the closest thing I could find, usually my oldest sister, Glenda.

"Get your paws off my little brother!" she'd yell like those lions I'd heard at the Tulsa Zoo. My troubles were solved . . . for a while.

After three or four times of me runnin through the broken porch door hollerin for someone to save me, Mama put a stop to the fistfights with one good twig from the biggest willow in our front yard and one good buck-naked ass.

I didn't even want to watch no boxing match that night. I wanted to throw the football around with a few of my neighbor friends — it really didn't matter that it was 28 degrees and the middle of February.

But somethin crawled into the drafty old house that winter night of 1964. I call it the Spirit of God. I call it God's will. Because of it, I'd never be the same.

"I am the greatest! I'm gonna put that ugly bear on the floor and after the fight I'm gonna build myself a pretty home and use him as a bearskin rug. Liston even smells like a bear."

I loved these strange words comin out of this good-lookin black athlete's mouth. It was a confidence and a teasin that I hadn't seen from a fighter before, specially a black man. He was playin with Liston like some kid's toy — teasin, teasin, never backin off, even though he didn't have no chance.

"It's gonna go so far down his throat," Liston bragged about his left fist, "that it'll take a week for me to pull it out again." We believed him. We'd seen what Liston could do with Floyd "The Rabbit" Patterson and "Big Cat" Cleveland Williams.

So who was this other black guy on the screen claimin to be the greatest? He was gettin ready to step into the ring with a heavyweight monster — a monster who'd beaten the crap out of plenty of fighters.

Ding. Round one. "And Clay steps toward Liston . . ."

Somethin about that fight pulled me in, like I couldn't see nothin else, like some magician was workin a trance on me, drawin my eyes to Clay's every move. The feet, so quick and full of life, flyin in the air like those hummingbirds I'd seen outside my living-room windows in the summer. His quick jabs that I'd miss if I blinked, his head movement, side to side, dodgin Liston's left jab, and another, and another.

"I wanna be like him, Jerry," I heard my voice say to my step-father, just kinda whisperin. But nobody paid me no attention. Jerry just kept his eyes glued on the set, boxin in the air once in a while, Mama tried to get some sewin done on my brother's bluejeans, and my five sisters were punchin at each other. "Get 'im, Clay. Knock that sucka out, Clay!" Jerry yelled.

"I wanna . . . ," I tried again.

"You what?" asked Mama with her gentle smile.

"I wanna be . . ."

"THAT A WAY, CLAY! GO FOR THE JAW!"

"I can't believe what we're seeing here, can you? No one expected anyone to look so good against Liston," exclaimed the commentators.

"I . . . I . . ."

"CLAY'S THE MAN! CLAY'S THE MAN!"

"I . . . wanna . . . I wanna . . . I wanna be LIKE HIM! I WANNA BE CASSIUS CLAY!" I yelled at the top of my lungs, arms spread high above my head, the white baby teeth still in my mouth shinin like a toothpaste commercial.

"Ah, go awn and sit yourself down, Junior," scolded my sister Glenda. "I can't see with you squawkin and jumpin around like that."

"That's nice," said Mama. "You can be whoever you want to be. Just be quiet now so we can all watch the fight."

I knew nobody thought I was really serious. Sure, little kids think lots of things. They want to be cowboys, cops, firemen. Some want to be just like Daddy, if they have one. But that night Clay kept me from gettin discouraged. If he could do it, I could do it.

The fight kept goin. Round two, round three, round four, with the Tillises huddled close to Liston's and Clay's every black-and-white move. Clay movin clockwise around the ring, Liston hittin Clay with a body shot, a left in the ribs, a forceful jab at the face. But even with Liston's reputation of bein able to actually lift a fighter off the ground with his left jab, he couldn't get close to Clay.

Round five. Blood smeared along Liston's jaw, Vaseline and slimy snot mixed together under his nose and ran down his chin. Clay's shiny muscles wrapped around Liston's waist, exhausted but determined. Liston was gettin beat.

I knew, as I stared at the man not many people believed in,

that I wasn't alone. I had Cassius Clay on my side. I didn't have to be no black man who picked up his food stamps every month or died at 19 from a neighborhood bullet in his head. I wasn't gonna be like my friends who were just gonna do little things because they thought little. I was thinkin big things now and I knew who was on my side — Cassius Clay and God Almighty.

Ding. Round six. A left hook into Liston's head. BAM, BAM. Another. Liston's soggy mouthpiece flew through the air like one of them white flags in the war movies I seen on television, surrenderin. The fight was over.

Liston fell on his stool, his cornerman by his side. "No more, no more," he told the man rubbin him down. "No more. . . . I quit."

The crowds at the fight were shocked. Their boy, Sonny Liston, beaten by some cocky jerk who claimed to be the king of the world.

Clay couldn't have been more alive, even though he'd just gone six rounds with the heavyweight champion of the world. "I'm the king of the woooorrrrrrlllllllllddddddd," he shouted at the cameras and the Tillises. "Ain't I pretty."

Sportswriters and newsmen swarmed around that man, my new idol, who puffed around the ring like a peacock showin off his stuff. Microphones and bright camera lights shoved through the smoke to get close to Clay. "Eat your words!" he screamed in their faces, all the time smilin to himself as he played with them. "Ain't I pretty!"

No one in that small, dark living room on Virgin Street knew what was goin on in my little black head that famous night when Cassius Clay beat Sonny Liston, but I knew. I knew God was talkin to me through that man. God gave me a message that night I still remember. *"You will be a boxer — you will be in the ring of champions."* I was thinkin big now.

# CHAPTER 2

# FROM THE ROPE TO THE RING

Bein a cowboy has always been my first love, with boxing comin in a close second. Sometimes I feel like I was born in the wrong times. All this fast lifestyle of the '90s, with cars zoomin down highways, drivers talkin on their cellphones, and no time to just shoot the breeze. Give me a sorrel quarter horse, with a hot summer Oklahoma trail, a bandanna to wipe my brow once in a while, and a dip of water from a horse's trough, and I'd be livin high. I know where this cowboy love comes from — my great-grandfather, Uncle Pete we called him. He was a hell of a hand — that's cowboy talk for a "true" cowboy. I owe him my life for that piece of cowboy he left in me.

Uncle Pete, Peter Hawkins, lived to be 100 years old, born in 1865, died in 1965; his father, I been told, had been a slave, livin to be 122 years old. I guess they both knew how to live right, seein all the hard times they beat — slavery, poverty, the Dust Bowl, the Great Depression. Man! We could all stand to learn somethin from these men.

My great-grandfather was part Choctaw, and though his skin was a deep, rich black, he had the features of an Indian, with high cheekbones and those dark eyes that could stare right through ya. Uncle Pete married a short, round, full-blood Choctaw woman with two long silver braids hangin down to her elbows, touchin the dirty white apron that she always liked to wear.

Pete must have been tied to the Oklahoma land of the Choctaws even more than his full-blooded wife, Mary, because every Sunday he insisted on ridin his red sorrel to Fountain Baptist Church, the Indian church that stands to this day and is known to be the oldest church still runnin in Oklahoma. Rain or shine, sticky summer heat or wintry, icy, chilled-to-the-bone cold, Uncle Pete would get up at 5 a.m. every Sabbath day, slide on a pair of old cotton pants, ratty long underwear, then a second pair of ragged pants, a second shirt, this time maybe a checkered cowboy shirt, and another, and another, and another, and another. By the time the cock crowed, Great-Grandfather would have SIX pairs of pants on and SIX shirts, and no one knows how many pairs of socks he'd slide up his skinny legs before loadin himself into his cowboy boots.

He used to say, "What'll keep you warm in the winter'll keep ya cool in the summer." And it wasn't just on Sundays that he'd carry around such a load on his 5′5″ body; it was every day. The townspeople who're still alive to share their memories of Peter Hawkins will tell ya the same thing. What's so amazin, though, is that he never had a foul smell. And it gets me how an old man like that could wander all around the countryside on his big ole horse without knockin people over.

Uncle Pete would put his six layers on, load up the black plastic raincoat he always carried on the back of that horse even when there wasn't a cloud in the sky, and head off toward the old Indian church 13 miles away, a stained cowboy hat plastered to his head, a left cheek full of cheap tobacco. Plop, plop, plop, him and Nip would go, out from the bottoms where he lived with his six children and Choctaw wife, through the small town of Gibson Station, past the cotton farms of his relatives. It must have taken him several hours to get that far goin that speed, but Uncle Pete was never in a hurry. He got his joy from hearin a meadowlark callin out across the prairie or seein a hawk glidin over him lookin for a field mouse to snatch up. Bloop, bloop, bloop, old Nip would go, fartin along the grassy trail that was all smashed down, carryin his master to the small Indian church where he'd worship with the Choctaws and Cherokees.

My 80-year-old friend Selma Mosley remembers those days real good. She was only eight years old then, so when she got invited by a friend to go to this strange Indian church, she got excited. "Back then," she tells me, "most of the colored folk would go to St. John Baptist Church. We didn't know nothin bout no Indian church. So I was mighty curious."

When she arrived by hitchin a ride in her friend's bumpity wagon, Selma knew somethin weird was goin on, somethin excitin. All around the whitewashed wooden church were these huge cast-iron pots with steam rollin off them. "I'd never seen so much food — fried chicken, pork ribs, fresh chocolate cakes covered with white velvet icing, all spread out on old picnic tables — but it was those pots that really bothered me. 'What was them pots and what was boilin inside of them?' I remember thinkin."

Not too long ago we both found out that those pots were probably full of three different kinds of favorite Choctaw dishes — holhponi (hominy corn), tanfula (hominy corn with beans, also called "Tom Fuller" by the Choctaws), and tanchi labona (hominy corn with pork meat). Every fall them Indians would get together for some kind of church meetin where they like to eat that hominy stuff, dance with those feathers on their heads, and elect officers for their tribe. Selma had walked right into a real live Choctaw ceremony.

There must have been the Choctaw storytellin blood in

Great-Grandpa, because I remember him tellin me wonderful stories when I was just a boy of five. I'd crawl up on his padded leg, wipe off the spiderwebs from the stale vanilla wafers he'd given me, feel his strong, callused hands wrap around my bony shoulder, and look into those Hershey-chocolate eyes. I couldn't wait to hear what he was gonna tell me.

"Back when I was younger, Junior, I got to ride with the cowboys. We'd break them horses so's we could ride 'em, then we'd brand those damn cows, and drive 'em to ranches all over the country. We'd be gone for months at a time. Your Great-Grandma use ta chew me out for bein gone so long, but that's the life of a cowboy, ya know.

"Me bein Choctaw and everythin, I was the one who'd talk to the Indians on the way. Creek, Choctaw, Cherokee. I remember meetin Frank and Jesse James, the Dalton Gang, the Youngers. One night we heard a man come scramblin off his horse into our camp, all huffin and puffin and stuff. Found out later he robbed a bank close by and a posse was out after 'im. We was all just bedded down for the night and he seen all us coloreds by our fire so he just lied there between us, lookin all cozy and everythin, jus part of the coloreds.

"Well, no fool in that white man's posse was gonna bother theirselves with a bunch of coloreds, so when they seen us camped out, they didn't even mess with us. Never did hear if that outlaw got what was comin to him but ya can't blame someone for usin his head like that."

It was stories like those that made me want to be around Uncle Pete. I was like a moth wantin to fly into some blinkin light. I was just a child, but for me, the light of the pioneer days, the cow-ropin days, and the olden days of Oklahoma Indians gave me the goosebumps. A lot of boys like to play cowboys and Indians, but for me it was different. I wasn't playin. I thought I was there with Jesse James and Uncle Pete the cowboy and the rest of them.

There was this pride in who you was back then, no matter if you was black or white or Indian red. Though Pete spent most of his time drivin cattle in the late 1800s, he later ended up with a whole lot of land for a black man, over 200 acres. I've heard he got some of that through the Oklahoma Land Run and then later from the government since he was part Choctaw, but lucky for him, he had some oil on that rich, fertile land they called the bottoms. He'd grown up with Oklahoma while it was growin up. He'd run cattle across her plains, he'd staked out a claim on her Verdigris River like his full-blood Choctaw neighbors would do, he'd built some of the first-ever railroad tracks, he'd become friends with the native Choctaw, Creek, and Cherokee people, and he'd finally enjoyed her rich, black gold.

My uncle used to tell me that Uncle Pete had buried a lot of money down by the pond on his land, so every day the ole man would ride Nip down there just to check on it. No wonder people still speak of old Pete as a proud man ridin his horse everywhere, always ridin with a place to go. He'd worked hard and he made damn sure he could enjoy it for all his 100 years. No white man, no new state government was gonna take nothin from him.

I'm not sayin he wasn't poor or nothin or that he had no enemies, because I've heard stories of such things. His daughter, Loreen, who we call Aunt Rena and who is 85 now, has told me what it was like to be one of his kids. "My daddy used ta hide his guns behind the walls of our house," she remembers, pointin a skinny black finger in the air, her dark eyes lookin like brown M&Ms. "Folks was always after him, tryin to steal his money. Once they shot up our house and messed it up real bad like. But Daddy ain't bothered by it. Every time he'd go to town, he'd come back with a big ole bag of candy, enough for us kids. The high yellas'd be shootin at him but he never got shot. He jis ride his horse outta the way."

There were other stories, too. Stories of voodoo — "hoodoo," Aunt Rena calls it. People would sometimes gather somethin called butterfly root, a flower that has a yellow top on it, which could be used for good or for bad. If somebody was after you, they'd use it to make an enemy sick; if they liked you, they'd use it "for good," to make a tea that could fix abdominal pains. They'd also burn hogs' hooves for good or for bad. The bad could poison you, the good could cure pneumonia.

Aunt Rena believes what she's heard for all these years. "Let me tell you this, Junior," she lectures me as soon as she's figured out that I'm Rosie's boy. "Don't get in bad with ya kinfolk. They all want my money and they tryin to poison me. They put lipstick on me one time and that lipstick had poison on it. It went straight to ma heart. They put poison in one girl's sloppy joe one time cuz they didn't want her to marry in. I knows they sneak in here every other night and try to poison me. I heared the lock on that door." She points past the box fan crankin in the window and over the faded dish towels throwed over her one lamp and her dusty stereo.

"One time they had me takin 20 pills for my pains and I said, 'You show me those people who takes these pills. They all either dead or ailin theyselves.' I can still taste those pills through my body. It takes a spoon of that castor oil to get it out. That's why my feet is swelled up to my knees. That's why I hafta sleep sittin up on this couch every night."

When Great-Grandpa was 100 years old, just before he died, he offered to build his daughter Loreen a house. How many 100-year-old men do you know? I've only known about two.

But how many 100-year-old men do you know who would want to start buildin a house? Most of them just want to sit in their wheelchairs.

Back in the early 1900s, people would build what they had cash to build — and that usually meant one room at a time. That's how Pete built his house, and he wanted to do the same for his daughter. Whatever would make her happy. But her house never got put up, and Pete's house finally burned down, after it was condemned and some burnin trash lit fire to it. Uncle Pete was mighty proud of that house and that land, though. He'd claimed that land by the river, and planted corn, wheat, and cotton on it.

Selma, who'd visited Great-Grandpa's church, remembers goin to the bottoms with her mama to see his family. "We didn't visit much folks in the bottoms but that's where the Hawkins people lived. I'd never seen such a place. Instead of just dogs tied up outside, Mr. Hawkins had two or three big ole hogs staked out in the front yard. That was the funniest thing I'd ever seen. Their house was made of wood, nice enough, but it looked kinda funny cuz it was all spread out, a real long, skinny house. I guess Mr. Hawkins jus kept addin rooms, one at a time. We'd go down into the bottoms where the trees growed everywhere, all shady and nice, and pick us some wild strawberries. They was growin everywhere. Plump, red, juicy berries. They had them some good land down there."

That kind of livin jus makes me want to turn a knob on one of them time machines you see in the movies and go back there. Sure, I know they was poor, but hey, so was I. The stuff about them usin paper sacks, corn cobs, leaves, anythin they could find for toilet paper jus makes me laugh. I know Uncle Pete had to boil all six pairs of his pants and six shirts every week in lye soap. But life was so simple back then, not all cluttered like it is today. People was people and they just enjoyed bein together.

Even though I was a little boy when Uncle Pete died, I still remember the funeral. It was real sad. Pete was layin there in the casket, his tired old hands folded across his chest, his shriveled black cowboy face restin on a plump white pillow, glad to be movin on to another world. All my kinfolk was there, slowly movin in single file down the church aisle, past the cheap wooden coffin and the little white funeral-director woman. The choir members were dressed in their finest, the big black women glad to have a chance to wear their fancy hats and high-heeled shoes as they sang "What a Friend We Have in Jesus."

I remember the wailin. Lots of wailin and moanin like the Good Book talks about on the Day of Judgment. I was only eight years old but my cousin Loraine was cryin big buckets on my shoulder.

"Don't be wearin me down, Miss Loraine," I remember tellin her, a kid's way of comfortin a boo-hooing woman. "He's dead now. Let him go." I just didn't get it.

I'll never forget seein six women all standin together at the back of the church, carryin on with their howlin and sobbin. "Who's them ladies?" I asked Mama, thinkin they was kin but not rememberin ever seein them at no family gatherins before.

"Shhhhh, don't you mind them, Junior," she said as she shushed me away with the backside of her big hand.

Well, it wasn't until I was about 16 that I figured out who those fine ladies were. Ole Pete Hawkins had him some women on the side that he'd been doin it to. *That crazy, dirty old man.* I wonder if each of them women knew she was one of a whole bunch. Johnny Lee, my second cousin, remembers Uncle Pete once goin out with a 45-year-old woman when he was 95, just 50 years older. He took her out for a candlelight dinner and they each had two glasses of wine that night.

"I sure would like for you to be mine," he told that pretty little young thing. So I guess they went to her house and made love.

"Johnny," Pete told him later, "I hooked my toes at the end of the bed and started workin as hard as I could. Oh! I was workin!"

"After an hour and a half went by, that little lady said, 'Peter Hawkins, ain't you ever gonna be through?'"

"I told her, 'Baby, I stopped gettin through 21 years ago. I'm makin love now.'" Sounds just like him.

So it was quite a scene watchin the people walk past Uncle Pete's body, those six women and even the kids actin like they'd lost their mamas. I guess that a lot of the children who was there had never looked at a dead person before, so when they was forced by their mamas and daddies to hold their hands and file by the coffin, it was too much. Kids and adults alike would walk up, peek in, then let out this scream that made my blood go cold. Aaaaaaaaaaaaaagggggggggghhhhhh! And as if the screamin and wailin wasn't enough, then some kid would pass out, hittin the floor with a thud.

Selma remembers it, too. "I was in the choir at Mr. Hawkins' funeral, so I was gettin a grand view of all them people goin by the coffin. I'd see the look of shock in those children's eyes, then those eyes would roll back into their heads, and they'd hit the flo. They was fallin out everywhere. So me and some others in the choir went up there and stood behind them, waitin for the scream, then catchin 'em when they was fallin out. I remember carryin one of his daughters out in her pretty blue dress. It was a real sad funeral, that one was."

Though I got my cowboy blood from Great-Grandpa Pete

Hawkins, it was his son, Theodore Hawkins, who everyone called Jack, that I got my athlete abilities from. Talk about country. He was more country than a pan of cornbread. Grandpa was a big old nigger who must have weighed at least 300 pounds, and his wife, Olivia, was just as big. He'd chop cotton all durin the week, and then on Sundays after church he'd head to the baseball field and pitch ten innings easy. When he was up to bat, he'd knock that ball clear out of the field. My mama told me that he had a chance to play for the Kansas City Monarchs back in the '30s, but I guess he wanted to be with his family instead.

Grandpa was known as a country pimp, even durin his married days. The farm boys told me that he'd make love to the chickens, cows, goats, horses, mules, and sheep because there wasn't no girls down in the country. Uncle Isom Hopkins told me that one night when Jack and Olivia slept in an upstairs bedroom at his house, he woke up to quite a ruckus goin on up there. The whole house was shakin, the sound of bedposts creakin, mattress springs squeakin. I guess 600 pounds of makin love will wake up just about anyone. Uncle Isom used to lie there in bed with his wife, listenin to all the commotion. When the gruntin and heavin would stop, Isom'd roll over on his pillow, and with a big grin on his face and a chuckle under his breath he'd say, "He's through now. We can go to sleep." And with that, the house would go back to dreamin.

Kids in school had heard stories about my country roots and it was just too temptin to see what they could get away with. That's where the stories about me started.

One mornin while we was stayin at my aunt and uncle's house, my cousin Jerry and I was wantin breakfast. Problem was, my Aunt Juanita and Uncle Melvin never had no money, so they couldn't buy many groceries. They never had nothin to eat and for me, a 13-year-old, and my cousin, an 11-year-old, that was a real nightmare. They would eat breakfast at noon and dinner at ten at night to stretch out the food. Man! We were some hungry, growin boys and we needed somethin in our bellies. So when Jerry and me found some outdated cornchips and Doritos in the barrel where Uncle Melvin put his crunchy snacks for the hogs and cows, I decided to eat my stale treasure in the barn, where no one would steal any.

Tammy, my cousin, came lookin for me but I jumped back in the barn because I didn't want her to beg off me. I was hidin in that stinky, stale hay, suckin on stale Doritos, real quiet and all, layin there beside my uncle's calf, whose navel cord was still hangin down, and I thought, "Hey, I bet that fool stole that calf from somewhere." Well, too bad for me, that silly-lookin calf died that night. After my kinfolk found out I'd been in the barn that same day, they decided to have some fun.

"Well, Junior, either you made love to that calf of Melvin's or you killed him," they teased me.

The next day, my brother-in-law, Lewis Payne, picked me up at my aunt's house in his red 1964 Barracuda. He had this funny look on his face, like he knew somethin I didn't.

"Junior." He had this twinkle in his eye and a silly grin on his face. "You been makin love to those cows in your aunt's barn?"

"What? What?" I asked, not believin my ears. "Somebody's been feedin you some shit," I told him. "You don't know what you're talkin about." He asked me again and again and I kept tellin him the same thing. But that crazy story was just beginnin. Later my mother asked me if it was true, and my cousins, and sure enough, some of the kids at school.

Five years later, I figured that fool story about the calf was long gone. But I was wrong. I was gettin ready for the Olympic trials. In 1976 I was one cool dude, feelin pretty proud that I was goin so far in boxing. I was walkin down the hall at McLain High School in my Sunday best — black leather jacket, Banlon long-collared shirt, double-knit pants, and high-heeled, stacked shoes — when Chiquite Foster comes up to me, all nice and cutesy.

"Hey, James, I hear you been gettin it on with those horses of yours," she said with this whiny little know-it-all voice.

"Bitch, what you say?" I asked her. Then I jumped at her, ready to beat the tar out of her stupid little head.

Her cousin, Sherry Barnes, who was standin right there takin it all in, said, "You bet not hit her. I'm gonna tell Sam."

"Who the hell is Sam?" I asked.

"That's her brother Dale," she warned.

Hey, a brother named Dale who goes by Sam was nothin for me who'd won the Regional Golden Gloves two years in a row and was now trainin for the Olympic trials.

"Yeah, right. I'll kick his ass," I told all the kids who was gatherin around us by now.

The next day at noon, lunchtime for most, I was rugged with my Golden Gloves jacket, my fancy Converse tennis shoes, and my bluejean overalls. Man! I had come to school to fight. But Dale-called-Sam was hopin I'd forgot.

Then I saw him. Walkin in with his Sunday best on, too uppity for a fight. After he seen how mad I was gettin and how pumped the crowd was for a fight, he ran home to change. It was fightin time.

I stood on the holy school emblem in the middle of the hall by the front door, its words "loyalty, honor, determination" lookin so pretty engraved on the floor under my size-12 feet. I was up for this. After a few minutes, the back door opened and

I saw him comin down the hall, his stiff black hair all braided tight, wearin his blue jeans and tennis shoes. The clothes of a school soldier.

He walked up to me. "What's that shit you been talkin?"

Well, from what I figured it was him and his sister who'd been doin the talkin, so I was all out of patience.

BAM! I hit him with a left lead. I was fightin southpaw at that time, so I caught him good. He staggered . . . staggered, then the riot broke loose. His friends came at me, knockin me in the jaw. Somehow a friend and my cousin Gerald grabbed Sam's friends and dragged those niggers down the hall to do their own fightin.

It was my time to shine. I hit him with some good combinations. Right jab, left cross, right hook. He'd try to go up under me, but I used to be a wrestler and I knew those moves. I'd pancake out and put him in a half-Nelson, while the same sister who caused the fight in the first place kept hittin me in the back with the closest weapon she could find — a cake cutter, one of those combs we used to use for our sticky, poofed-out Afros. Finally, after I'd had enough of her beatin me with that thing and him throwin punches at me, I turned around and crowned her ass. She was the school queen that year — crowned by the school and crowned by me.

I never heard any more rumors about me and my country cows or horses after that. I guess my friends and kinfolk thought it wasn't worth all the fun.

"You know, people say I make love to cows, chickens, goats, and sheep. Well, guess what? I'll do it to you!" I'd tell anyone messin with me. That shut 'em up. Shut me up too. I got suspended for ten weeks after that school riot and had to go to some alternative school to learn my lesson.

Yeah, I got that country love from Great-Grandpa, but that love for fightin, the strength, reflexes, timin, coordination, balance, speed, and a hell of a will to win all came from Grandpa. I guess we all have a little of someone deep in our blood. I'm just glad Peter Hawkins and Theodore Roosevelt Hawkins have some of them in me.

CHAPTER 3

# CORN WHISKEY AND BOOTLEGGING MY DADDY

When Glenda was born, my daddy said, "OW! A girl!" When Olivia was born, he said, "OW! Another damn girl!" When Sheryl was born, he said "F*#!&, another girl!" When Penny was born, he said "Son of a *b*#!&*, another girl!" But, in 1957, on the day after our country had celebrated its independence, the same date that my father had been born, July 5th, another miracle of independence took place — seven pounds of all boy, James Tillis, Jr., pushed his way into the Tillis family of girls.

Daddy got the phone call when he was carvin pork loin from the bone, back in the butcher shop of the famous downtown Mayo Hotel.

"Is this Mr. James Tillis?" he heard a voice say on the other end of the line.

"Yeah, it sure is," Daddy said, thinkin the restaurant manager upstairs needed another order of brisket.

"Your wife Rosie just had her a little boy."

"Damn! Who're you kiddin?"

A few hours later, my daddy was stone drunk with his brother-in-law, Sylvester Hooks.

"After we got smashed," said Syl, the name only his good friends are allowed to call him, "I helped him sober up a bit and we took off for the Morton Hospital where Rosie was."

"Let me see between his legs!" Mr. Tillis yelled out when he got to Mama's room. No "Hey, baby, how ya feelin?" or "I'm so proud of ya, baby." No, my daddy needed evidence.

"What do you think of your new son?" asked the white doctor as he stopped by on his usual rounds.

"Damn! That kid's got a hell of a set of nuts on him!" Drunk or sober, my father had found a new pride in life. He had a son — a son who would be the hero he never was.

My daddy had lots of love for lots of things — his kids, his wife, his friends, his wine, and his 50-cents-a-pint corn whiskey. Thunder Bird, Chock (that home brew made in someone's kitchen), Night Train, Ripple, Ariba, Mad Dog, Jim Beam, Kentucky Gentleman — he could drink the hell out of those wines and whiskeys, always tryin to give a nip here and there to his only son. But you know, probly by the grace of God, I never had no taste for whiskey. Tastes like shoe polish to me.

When I was a little kid about five years old, Daddy would wake me up in the middle of the night, grab my hand proudly in his, and off we'd go to the bootleggin joints of north Tulsa, me still wipin the yellow sleep out of my eyes. He wanted to make sure I wouldn't turn out to be no sissy or nothin, not with all them girls in the house.

So me and Daddy would walk past the Greenwood businesses and churches, all closed up for the night, the owners sleepin in their beds, where I should have been. Daddy'd be walkin fast, ready for what was ahead. Me? I was draggin my feet, wonderin how many drunks I'd see in the alleys that night. We'd walk by the Church of the Lord Jesus Christ, the Red Light Shine Parlor, Ida Bell's Tavern, Elliott's Shoe Shine, and the plumbing supply store, White Nipple Company. It was Greenwood Street in all its '60s glory.

Finally, we'd walk past the drunks, who smelled like cheap

corn whiskey, in their dirty, buttonless coats, through the back-yard into Jack Rens' or Pete Child's, Hip Worrie's, Ike and Mary's, or Mrs. Tillie's. I still remember hangin out in the back rooms of those joints at 3 a.m. Fancy clubs like the Four-Twenty-Five Club and the Calypso Room that sold liquor by the "wink" had already shut down, so some people would sell the hard stuff in the back of what they called houses — but they was really just a few boards with a tin roof. My sister Glenda called them "gamblin shacks." As long as nobody started fights, they could run for years without the cops botherin them.

Yeah, we were livin it up all right. On the backstreets of Greenwood, where just 40 years earlier hundreds of blacks had been hurt or killed in the famous 1921 Tulsa Race Riots, J.T. Tillis was thinkin he'd make a little history himself. Daddy drinkin, me watchin and shakin my head. "Lord, have mercy, Lord, have mercy," I'd say in my little-kid voice, not seein why anyone would want to get so tore down with shoe polish.

People ask me if I was real embarrassed or ashamed watchin Daddy get drunk in those joints. Hey, I was too little to know any different. All I cared about was that my daddy thought I was big enough to hang out with him. Twenty-five years later, I'd be in a similar juke joint, but this time it would be on a Steven Spielberg set, an overweight Oprah Winfrey sittin on my lap, all of us laughin and carryin on while we filmed *The Color Purple*. Sittin there on my favorite barstool at Jack Rens' place, though, in Tulsa, Oklahoma, I knew I could be more than he was ever gonna be. I had higher hopes and though he'd always love me, he'd try to drag me down deeper into his dirty hole of losers, not even knowin what he was doin.

Later when I got to junior high, he'd embarrass me for real. The Carver Cats, my junior-high football team, was playin the Anderson Hummingbirds. It was early October in 1970 and that excitin football feelin was in the air. The Cats huddled, callin the runnin number-two hold — we were ready to spit those birds out of our mouths as soon as we could.

"HUT! HUT!"

"Tillis, there go your daddy," my cousin Greg Hawkins said under his breath, sittin with me on the sidelines, waitin for some defensive action.

*Oh, man! Help me, Lord!* I was dreadin the sight of Daddy anywhere in public, except for the Greenwood bars.

Sure enough, there was my daddy for all the world to see. A bright lime-green jumpsuit with a big pee stain right on the front of his pants. I was gonna be the joke of every Cat and Hummingbird lineman, every friend in the stands, and specially my girlfriend, Charity Horne.

"Go awn, J.T., go awn!" I heard my mother call out to him as he swaggered up the stadium steps. My proud Mama could hardly take the shame; they was shakin their heads all disgusted and crackin jokes behind her back. "Get awn outta here, J.T."

He turned around, tryin to figure out where he was and why he was there, then tried to go back down the stairs, only to trip and fall. Bump, bump, bump, he rolled down those concrete steps like a tire bouncin off the back of some truck. When he finally hit bottom, somehow not breakin his skull wide open, he lifted himself off the cracked pavement like he was in slow motion.

"Hell, that didn't hurt none."

It was like the whole Carver Cats side was watchin Bill Cosby or somethin. HA, HA, HA. HA, HA, HA.

Out he came, father of defensive end James Tillis, Jr., grabbin me around the neck like I was his only pal. "This is my boy!"

"No, I ain't." I was really embarrassed now, pushin him back with my arm.

"Yes, you is," he shot back. Then he went through the whole list of women he loved — his wife and all her sisters — to show that nothin could compare to his love for that only son. "I like Rose, Margie, Jewel, Mildred, Ella, I like all of 'em but Junior here is MY boy." Then he walked out to the field, pulled out his black penis and peed on the fifty-yard line.

"Oh, MAN!" I cried out. I couldn't believe it and neither could all the other 200 spectators, their mouths hangin open in shock. Men was fallin off their wooden benches laughin, the women had their hands over their mouths and eyes.

After J.T. finished his business, he shook off the dew, put it back in his pants, and walked off, proud to be the father of his only son.

The game finally ended, 14–6, Hummingbirds over the Cats. When Coach White huddled together with his beaten Cats, squattin on one knee and talkin about what we did wrong, Edward Anderson said in his low, goofy voice as he looked at the man standing by himself deep in the end zone, "Look at Tillis's daddy!" I shot hooky for two weeks after that game. My girlfriend quit me and everythin.

My father wasn't around at home much when I was growin up; he just liked to step into my life once in a while and embarrass the hell out of me. But my sister Sheryl tries to remember the better times.

"We had some great times on Virgin Street before Daddy started his drinkin," she tells me as we sit by Daddy in his wheelchair at a Tulsa nursing home, watchin him rub his achin arm. "Daddy was makin $60 a month at the Mayo Hotel; Mama was doin day work, cleanin houses for people. Our rent was $50 a month, but somehow we made it. I don't believe we ever missed a meal. Daddy's big band music would sing through the house, saxophones and clarinets swayin through them cheap walls and across the plates of collard greens, but those were happy times.

"I remember when Daddy and Mama would go out on the town once in a while on Saturday nights. They liked to get dressed up in the same kind of outfits and stroll downtown together. Mama with her red bandanna around her neck, blue-jeans on her round body, and Daddy wearin just the same. They'd be so cute in those days. They'd leave us girls alone with Junior . . . didn't need babysitters in those days. Daddy knew our big ole Great Dane, Bo, would be all we'd need in the house."

Sheryl says that Daddy would bring home a bag of Fig Newtons and a toy for all the kids to share when he could. One toy don't seem like much to spoiled kids today, but it was plenty back then. Daddy brought home two toys, though, that would be more important to me than to any of my sisters — a plain little stick horse and one of them hobby horses that would rock back and forth. Boy, did I think I was somethin ridin that hobby horse or runnin around the neighborhood with that crazy stick horse, whoopin and hollerin. Whether it was because of Peter Hawkins, raisin me with them real horses, or that fake stick horse, the cowboy blood was always gonna run thick in me.

But somethin else was gonna be runnin thick in Daddy's blood — he had him a real drinkin problem. Man, he loved that corn whiskey.

When I was only five years old, Daddy left us. As Mama used to say, "Your daddy dropped us like a bad habit." I'll never forget the night he left. Mama decided she'd fix us some fried chicken for dinner to make us feel better and all.

"Junior," she told me that night. "You gonna be the man of the house now."

Well, with that news, I reached out across the table, all big and tough, and stuck my fork in a fat, juicy breast of chicken.

BAM. Mama backhanded me in the mouth like nothin flat.

"Nigger, you ain't THAT much man," she said. You never could get spoiled with Mama around.

Nothin brings me more joy than hearin stories of my kinfolk. And sometimes the people who remember things best about my daddy are the ones who'd hang out with him behind Mama's back and away from those sharp eyes of hers. Daddy's best friend and brother-in-law Sylvester Hooks tells the best stories of some pretty crazy times.

"Yeah, that ole J.T. could sure get mean and high-tempered when he drank," Syl remembers of his drinkin buddy. He's sittin in his livin room on a couch covered in plastic. "We was always hangin out together. I'd go by and pick him up to get him outta that house of women. The neighborhood bar was too full, so we'd park in my uncle's yard, get us a good parkin place that way, then walk down the street to Pig Al's."

Laughin under his breath, his rough gray and white hair stickin out in patches on the side of his head, lookin like Groucho Marx or someone, Sylvester shares a scary night he had with my daddy.

"We'd always head to Sapulpa to get drunk cuz back then there was no liquor stores around. Even though you could get the stuff in Tulsa, there was more police in the city, but just the sheriff in a small town. Had to grease too many palms in Tulsa.

"Ya see, before whiskey became legal in 1959, a lot of the hotshots, especially the cops, would get payoffs of $100 to $200 a month for keepin their traps shut while bar owners ran their businesses. If the owners didn't pay up, then they'd see the wrath of law and God. Sure enough, ole Tulsa Police Chief Paul Livingston and Police Commissioner Jay Jones, along with fourteen other cops, got convicted for bootleggin back in '57, when everyone else around here was celebratin the 50th anniversary of Oklahoma bein a state and all. Sent 'em off to the federal pen. Livingston had been gettin $500 a month easy from payoffs." He shook his head. "Too many people to pay off back then.

"Well, one night J.T. and me went to Sapulpa to get looped. I thought we was jus goin to one of our favorite night spots, which back then was a hangout in the back of a house or next to a run-down restaurant. After hours, the owners couldn't sell no liquor, so they'd use these hideaways to sell the stuff and make some profit. J.T. took me to some guy's house, and before I knew what was goin on, five of us was draggin out pints of good whiskey, three or four at a time, that was hidin in a dark, smelly crawl space under his house.

"'What the hell's goin on?' I asked J.T. and this crazy guy.

"'We jus robbed a whiskey still,' another guy I'd never seen told me. 'What, are you chicken or somethin?'

"Well, I don't want to look like no fool, so we kept draggin that bottled whiskey off the mildewed carpet it was sittin on. Hours must have gone by in that black night, cuz we ended up fillin the whole back end of my car with over 200 pints of whiskey.

"'That's enough, J.T. Let's get outta here,' I told him under my breath."

"You probly don't remember this, Junior," he tells me, eyes all wide like just tellin this story is makin it happen again, "but back then our license tags had the number 2 on the end of the tag if the car was outta Tulsa County, a 1 from Oklahoma City. Well, some white policeman saw our number-2 tag drive by at 2 a.m. and that's all it took.

"He shined his blindin flashlight in our eyes — J.T. sittin

beside me, three guys in the back, me drivin. 'What you boys doin out here this time a night? It's time to go to bed.'

"Well, back then those damn police would shine that damn flashlight in your eyes seein if you was drunk or not. Hell, by the time they was done shinin that bright light in your eyes, you'd look like you'd been drinkin all night.

"All I could think about, though, was them damn 200 pints of whiskey sittin on the back floorboard, an old rug thrown over them, with six legs sittin on top of that.

"The cop made me and J.T. get out and he could see right away that J.T. was drunk and actin crazy — he couldn't even stand up — so the cop made him, then me, walk the white line on the side of that country road. Guess who passed the test? I hightailed it outta there and J.T. got to spend a night or two in jail.

"But before I left, I asked J.T. real quiet so the cop couldn't hear me, 'Hell, J.T., what'm I gonna do?'

"'Hell, sell the damn whiskey!' was his only fool reply.

"I ended up drivin around scared half to death but finally found some other fool to buy all 200 pints. Paid me $1.50 a pint. Yeah, ole J.T. and me go way back. We was always lit up, actin like damn fools — two peas in a pod."

I'd heard the drunk stories and a few of the jail stories before, but I hadn't heard Sylvester's ghost story — his wife and J.T. didn't hear it either for a long time after it'd happened. Seems like there's stories of spirits floatin around a lot in my family. When Mama was nine years old, at the bedside of her dyin mother, she looked in the mirror and there was somethin lookin at her. What it looked like I don't know, but they say that spirit poisoned my grandmother. She died at the same time Mama saw the spirit in the mirror.

Sylvester still gets this Freddy Krueger look in his eyes when he talks about one night he took my daddy home; of course they both been drinkin, Daddy a lot more than Sylvester. But it was Sylvester who saw the woman.

She was walkin under the streetlight down from my house on Virgin Street. It was 2:30 in the mornin and Sylvester and J.T. was talkin about the bar fight they'd seen the night before. Just sittin there enjoyin the '52 Buick Syl'd bought a few months before, a convertible, shiny red and black.

"Who's that lady, J.T.?"

"What lady?"

Silence. "You don't see that lady down there under the street-light . . . the one with the dark dress on?" He gulped.

"Nah, you idiot. There ain't nothin down there. Ya better go awn home and git some sleep, Syl."

Well, Sylvester wasn't exactly thrilled about drivin down the hill past that lady under the streetlight, but he started to convince himself she was someone he knew — that single woman, Ramona, who lived a few houses down. He just couldn't figure out why she'd be walkin the neighborhood that time of mornin since she had a car. So Sylvester put his car in neutral, like he always did after droppin off my drunk Daddy, and started to coast down the hill so he could take a left easy around the corner, endin up in his driveway — not a peep, not a chug comin from his muffler. A sure way of not wakin up the neighbors, includin two angry wives who knew their husbands been out drinkin from 9 till 2:30 a.m.

"As I coasted past the lady in her black evenin gown, dressed like she'd been nightclubbin, I looked out my window at her. She just kept walkin past that light, starin straight ahead. She never even glanced at me . . . it was like she was in a trance or somethin . . . or like she wasn't even real."

When Sylvester passed her, he peeked in his rearview mirror

for one last look at the strange woman, the woman who might have been the new single lady in the neighborhood. But when he looked, she'd disappeared.

"Just like that," he told me. "One minute she was there, me coastin past her; the next minute, nothin. Whoa! I got me some big goose bumps on the back of my neck and thought to myself, 'Damn! Where'd she go anyway?'"

Syl went ahead and parked his car real quiet like in his driveway, then, bein all brave, tried to find the lady in the dark dress. He figured she took the shortcut between the houses across the street, the trail that kids had tromped down on their way to the neighborhood grocery store. "Hell," Syl said. "I knew I'd catch up with her cuz she couldn't have gone anywhere else."

But he didn't catch up with her. Couldn't find a damn thing. "I felt cold like a block of ice when I didn't see no sign of her. I ran for home as fast as I could, goin down that trail with my eyes half-closed." As he jumped in bed with his clothes on, he was tremblin, his heart racin like a freight train.

"Sylvester, what's gotten into you anyways? You shakin like ya seen a ghost," his wife, Jewel, said. The creak of the mattress springs and the gaspin of her husband's breathin woke her up.

"I tell you, Junior," Syl says now. "If she could have seen me in the dark of our bedroom that night, she'd a thought I'd turned into a WHITE man. My mama told me a long time ago that I was born with a veil over my face, meanin that I could see spirits. She used to say that I had a gift, that not everybody can see them, but that night I sure didn't feel like I had no gift. I was scared like hell. If I'd run into that lady again, I sure enough woulda died."

Sylvester never saw the mystery woman again, but several spooky things happened later. One night his four-year-old kid,

Chris, came runnin out of the back part of the house where he slept and jumped in bed with Syl and Jewel.

"Daddy, Daddy," he whispered, not wantin to wake up his mama. "Who's that woman in my bedroom? The one in the black dress?" He'd seen her, too — the family gift of "the veil."

"Syl! Syl!" Sylvester heard from the hall another night, when everyone was asleep. He checked to see who it was, but he didn't see nobody nowhere.

A few days later, Sylvester and Jewel was watchin TV when it just shut off. Suddenly a black cat appeared out of nowhere, his eyes sparklin like gold, and jumped through the livin room.

"Where'd that dang cat come from?" Jewel knew their family didn't have no kind of cat and never seen one black cat in the neighborhood.

Sylvester ran through the house to grab the cat but it'd just disappeared. Nothin.

"I looked everywhere and what I couldn't figure out was how that thing even got in. The front door was closed, all the windows was closed, the back door was shut tight with one of those two-by-fours dropped by it, ya know, Junior, what I'm talkin about. The way we used to bolt them back doors.

"But I never could find that cat and never saw it again. Some people told me later it was that lady in the dark dress. I guess it had to be her. We got the hell out of there soon after that. I ain't never told Jewel about any of this stuff till later. Good thing, too. We found out that a lady'd been stabbed to death by her boyfriend in the back room where my boys slept, just three months before we'd moved there. It was then I remembered that stain on the carpet and underneath on the floor that Jewel never could get out. Blood. Good thing that house got tore down soon after. Apartment complex sit there now. Yeah, good thing."

# CHAPTER 4

# A BAD
# LITTLE BOY

My cousins say I was the baddest kid on the block. Nobody wanted to come to my house and spend the night, nobody wanted to ride bikes with me, nobody wanted to play football with me. And there was a reason — I was a real bad little boy.

It was 1964 and Daddy had left us like a bad habit. Mama'd gotten married again to a guy named Jerry and they had them a girl, Angela, along with a son, Barry. She was tryin to make a livin for her seven kids, cleanin white people's houses in south Tulsa, the rich end of town. We lived on food that came from Uncle Sam in his red, white, and blue hat — USDA commodities. But when the big chunk of yellow cheese and the canned Spam ran out, the refrigerator stayed pret' near empty. For a growin boy, it seemed like it was always empty.

Maybe that's why I had such an attitude. I can at least try to blame it on me bein poor. I hated bein poor and I was always tryin to climb out of it. So I took it out on everybody else.

"If it didn't go Junior's way, he had to fight. He was real high-tempered," my cousin Ronnie Hawkins says. "It didn't make no difference if he was only eight or nine years old and the other guys were fifth and sixth graders. Junior was the baddest kid on the block and at school and he'd fight anybody for anything."

Ronnie and me would stay together a lot, either at his house or mine, along with the ten other kids of our combined families; his mama would drop off her five kids at our house when she went to do day work and my mama would drop us seven kids off at Ronnie's mom's house when she went to do her day work. Twelve kids, includin me and Ronnie, in one small house is askin for trouble.

It was a hot August day and Mama had kicked us all out of the house. "Go awn outside and play, get outta this house," she'd always tell us, no matter if it was a freezin February day covered with slushy ice or a humid August day with sweat drippin off the window screens. "Go awn now, you kids," she'd say.

We'd grab our nickels and head down to the Dairy Hut on 27th and Cincinnati. Just as we'd sat down one day on the hot bench in the parkin lot, I decided I didn't want Ronnie to get cooled off no more.

POW. I knocked that soft, cool chocolate Dairy Hut ice cream right off Ronnie's cone.

Ronnie usually played low when I was pickin a fight with him, but that did it. POW. Right when I was gettin ready to take a big ole lick of ice cream.

"Why, you #%&*#%!!" Arms goin everywhere, fists smackin each other's heads, stomachs, legs, anythin we could find that might hurt. After Ronnie grabbed my face and rubbed it in the "chatt," what we called the gravel of the parkin lot, I chased him home on my bicycle.

"Rosie! Rosie! Junior's after me! Junior's after me!" he yelled as he ran through that front door.

"Ya better not be fightin, Junior. You HEAR me?"

Ronnie stepped out into the yard, sure that he was safe, then saw me hidin behind the bushes with a wooden bat knockin real hard like against my open palm.

"I KNOW he's not gonna hit me with that bat," Ronnie remembers thinkin. And then he don't remember nothin.

WHOP! One blow to the arm and the next thing I knew, Mama was beatin my buck-naked little black ass. The willow switch again.

"Somethin bad's gonna happen to ya, somethin bad's gonna happen to ya," Ronnie shouted as he was driven off to the hospital. "You wait and see."

When Ronnie came back from the hospital a few hours later, with his arm in a sling — I'd fractured it in a few places — I ran out to see what damage I done. At the same time ole Billy Blue, the blackest kid on the block, was ridin his bike like a crazy kid who'd just seen him a ghost. Head down, legs peddlin round and round, round and round. He never saw me.

CRASH. Those shiny, probably stolen, handlebars of Billy Blue's banged right into my fat skull. I never knew what hit me but all I could hear while I was spread out on the ground in a fog was Ronnie's words, "You dead, Junior? You dead? I tole you that somethin bad's gonna happen to ya, I tole you." Me and Ronnie was a real sight that night — Ronnie in his sling, me with a big ole knot on the side of my head.

Ronnie used to bawl all the way down the block when he had to come spend the night with me. "Pleeeeaaaaasssse, Mama, don't make me stay with Junior. Pleeeeaaaaassse." I guess it didn't help none that I was always standin there on the front porch with my mean little face scrunched up in a snarl, my right fist shut tight and rammin into the palm of my left hand. Everyone was scared of Junior.

But there was another reason nobody wanted to spend the night with Junior. I liked to pee all over 'em in bed. Not on purpose, of course. I just couldn't help it.

"Don't peeeeee on meeeee, pleeeaaassse, Junior, pleeeaaasse don't peeeee. These are my last drawers," Ronnie would beg before Mama made us get in bed together.

"Get that plastic," she'd yell to Glenda, who was used to it by now.

But it'd happen every time. And Ronnie was my favorite pick of all the cousins. You'd think he could have just slept on the floor and been happy but "them rats runnin around on the floor scared me," he says. "I'd rather get soaked than have them rats crawl all over my legs."

Mama always left the window open in the bedroom for a nice fresh breeze, but by the next mornin, Ronnie and me would be shiverin in the lake of pee. Even though my cousin always tried to make himself a fort with a big ole thick bed-spread jammed between us, it didn't make no difference. I'd aim right at him and he'd wake up with this warm swiishh, swiisshhh all around him. Man, right through the fort.

"You just a pee-wee booooyyyyy, you juuuusssssttt a peeee-weeee boy," they'd all sing in the mornin, me ready to put someone else in a cast if they kept it up.

All of my ugly sisters like to remind me of the camp I went to when I was older — they say I was 15, but I say, you gotta be kiddin me, I was jus six. They lie a lot. Anyway, the stupid counselors had to show the whole world the next mornin that bad boy Junior wet the bed. Hanged the mattress with the big ole pee stain outside in front of my cabin. "You just a pee-wee booooyyyyy, you juuuusssssttt a peeee-weeee boy," I got from everyone, especially my sisters. They say I didn't quit peein all over the bed until I was 16. I say they're crazy fools.

Livin with all them girls, I had to act like a man, ya know. Really try to impress 'em by catchin flies with my hands, then stickin them on my tongue — head, wings, eyeballs, everythin. Real cool stuff like that. But sometimes I found out the hard way that I wasn't really ready for some grown-up things. I wasn't always the big man I thought I was, even at seven.

Ever since I can remember, I've liked to get up early. Now, I'm not talkin 7 or 8 o'clock like most kids on Saturday mornins; I'm talkin 5 or 6 a.m. every mornin. Even today if I sleep in too late, I feel like a homoSEXual or somethin, a sissy, layin there in bed with my eyes wide open, ya know, like those guys from Beverly Hills, makin curls for the girls and waves for the babes, wearin earrings and lotion. I'm a cowboy, ya see, and cowboys don't like all that sissy stuff. I've always loved to get up early and enjoy the mornin. And when I was a kid, the earlier the better. There was so much to do — work on my go-cart, walk in the junkyards and alleys lookin for bicycle parts, stuff that little boys like to do.

One day I'd gotten up early to run around the neighborhood a little to see what I could find. I'd grabbed me a few pop bottles from a front yard or two, then decided to make my way back home — I had some serious work to do on the go-cart I was tryin to put together. It didn't make no difference that it was only 30° outside and the middle of February. Bo, our Great Dane, and me was always workin together on my go-cart, him spread out on the ground, just glad to be sittin by somebody, me thinkin I was some kind of mechanic.

As I reached around behind me to grab Daddy's old yellow screwdriver so I could tighten the wheel, I felt a bunch of cold, matted hair. "Hmmmm, that's funny," I thought, since I was lookin right at Bo sleepin in front of me in the dirt. "And Bo doesn't have hair like . . . THAT! MAMA! MAMA! HELP ME! AAAAGGGGGGHHHH!" I screamed when I turned around and saw what my hand was holdin.

Behind me was a 95-year-old naked black lady with long, stringy gray hair frozen to her head. She was kneelin over, her scrawny arms crossed over her chest, tryin to keep warm. She didn't say nothin. Just stared. I guess Bo wasn't too worried about no naked frozen lady in our backyard, but it sure made me run quick to Mama for help.

That was the first naked lady I'd seen that wasn't in a magazine, but a few years later I got me even MORE of an eduCAtion. I'll never forget the day because I was out pickin up leftover firecrackers from the Fourth of July. It was July 5, 1965. My birthday. A real hot month, when everyone, at least in the colored section, had their windows open to get a breeze if they was lucky. I was out cruisin the neighborhood again to see what kind of trouble I could get into or what kind of cool stuff I could find. I figgered everybody was sleepin — all my sisters, my mama, my cousins, my friends on the block.

*Hey, what's the gruntin over there at that house?* I thought it was probly a couple of dogs chewin on a bone in my neighbor's backyard. *Better go check it out.*

I walked around the little house to find that gruntin. Didn't sound like no dogs now. Sounded like someone was in trouble. *Maybe I can help or somethin.*

Finally, I figured out where that noise was comin from — through one of the back windows that was wide open, just the broken screen hangin off the hinge a little. So I pushed my little feet up as high as they'd go on their tiptoes and peeked my little head into that window. The gruntin just seemed to get louder and louder, one low, growly noise like a mean bear, one higher noise like a kid gettin a whoopin. What I saw was my first lesson in sex education.

*So THAT'S how they do that! Wow! When I get big, I wanna do THAT.*

I must a stood there for five minutes before my foot slipped and made a noise. Man, that guy shot over to that window, but not as fast as I took off. That little lesson got me a whoopin from Daddy when I tried doin what I'd just seen to one of my sister's big ole dolls. That was the only whoopin he ever gave me. We still laugh about it when I go see him in the nursin home.

But it was the Carver Junior High days that really got me in big trouble. It didn't matter if high school boys wanted to fight me or if "Prof" Robinson, our gym teacher, wanted to whoop my ass. I was still a bad little boy, just gettin older.

"I like bread and butter
I like toast and jam.
But the thing I like most of all
Is to hear your butt go BAM!"

That was the rhyme Prof Robinson called out to me about every week — his idea of some cute poetry. We loved to tease 'im and call 'im "Prof" because he seemed so old to us kids and because he'd been there for so long, like he'd been born in 1840 or somethin. He'd get out that wooden paddle of his with holes in it and beat me till my ass was cooked like okra. My cousins always took up for me but they didn't want no part of the fightin — "Junior, please don't start . . ." "I ain't goin to do nothin," I'd go — and then I'd have two or three guys on me with bloody noses and broken arms.

"Junior, you couldn't hear some lip and keep on goin," my cousin Ronnie reminds me. "You just couldn't take no stuff."

Later, when I wasn't flunkin out of history at McLain High School or goin to Brother Floyd's, the store down the street, to get me a nickel biscuit or a bowl of beans for lunch, I'd be playin the dirty dozens, we called it; they call it "baggin" now.

"Tillis, your mama's got three titties. Smack. Crackle. And

pop," one smart dude would say.

"Hey, when my daddy and your daddy was playin in the grass, my daddy stuck his finger in your daddy's ass," I'd come back at him.

Back and forth, round and round we'd go. Seein who could outdo the other. We were bad, but man, we had us some fun times. Thing is, that's all I knew. Just havin fun, playin the dozens, beatin up on each other, tryin to forget we was all a bunch of losers with nothin better to do than talk bad about our drunk daddies and mamas.

But boxing saved me. I know you hear a lot of fighters say that, but it's true for me. If I hadn't been taught what to do with that attitude and how to use that meanness in a good way, I'm sure I'd be in jail today doin three years for assault — somebody givin me lip and me goin after him. But boxing taught me what to do with that athlete ability, that fightin drive inside me, and it made me see that what God had given me was a good thing. Boxing gave me the determination and discipline that many black kids need today. Boxing taught me character. I got to see the world. I got to meet all the great champs. Yeah, it saved me.

CHAPTER 5

# AMATEUR DAYS

The six of us stepped out of his white '65 Pontiac, the red-and-white terry cloth robes hangin real nice like over our arms, matchin vinyl bags in our hands. I was 16, in my prime. The thought of the glory road ahead was makin my blood pump fast through my veins — *wasn't nobody gonna mess with me.*

My friend Ronnie Warrior remembers that day like it was yesterday. It was 1974 at a smoker, a one-nighter of several fights in Henryetta, Oklahoma, at the Armory gym. Ronnie and his team were small-town guys from Okmulgee, with worn, faded things they called boxing gloves on their hands, hightop PF Fliers they called boxing shoes on their feet, and brown Safeway grocery sacks they called handbags.

"I was so embarrassed," Ronnie told me later, "when I saw you big Tulsa guys get out of that car with your fancy robes and fancy bags. We was just small-town guys with no money, just there to have fun. We didn't have a real trainer, just Piggy Brown, a guy who had trained himself how to fight. I'd never heard of this James Tillis everyone was talking about, but by the time the tournament started, we were ready to see what he could do."

Ronnie reminds me, though, that amateur boxing back then was not what it is today. Twenty years ago, the amateur teams would have a tournament every week in some town.

Tournaments might run three days — three rings one night, two rings the next, and one ring the last night. Today it's hard enough to find enough fighters for a smoker, a one-night show.

"We'd go three rounds then, same as today, but the qualifications of the boxers were much higher," says Ronnie, "so kids today could never have made it back then. Boxers who qualify for the Olympic teams today probably would have been second stringers at best. If Quick was in his early 20s today, he could have been world champ six times. It's easy street today.

"Boxing's become like a health class or something, like recreation. Boxers today are telling their trainers what to do, not the other way around, like it's supposed to be. Back then, kids grew to be men at an early age. They were fightin to get out of the projects or the Boys Clubs, off the streets. It took incredible determination to make it then. I'd say only three out of ten fighters today really have the determination to make it. Quick and me was only 16 but we were fighting MEN, big high-school dudes who could take on the professionals easy."

Some made it to the pros too. Harry Truman, "The President," made it, wavin his American flag around in the professional rings for all the world to see. Richard Cade, Jimmy Green, Michael Dokes, Greg Page. These were the kinda fighters Ronnie and me boxed in the ring.

And I'll never forget Leon Bruner — the two of us was the talk of the tournament that weekend in Henryetta. Black and goofy-lookin, with a silly grin on his face, 20-year-old Bruner looked just like big ole Jethro, Granny's grandson on *The Beverly Hillbillies*. Country as a pan of cornbread.

Ronnie remembers that day, me gettin ready to take on Bruner. "Tillis was the fastest kid I'd ever seen. When I saw him moving in the practice ring at age 16 like that, I knew he was trying to imitate Ali and he was damn close to him, even at that age. The foot speed, the hand speed, the way he slipped punches by sliding away from him. He even put his gloves up on the ropes like Ali."

Not many of the guys there had seen me fight. Everyone just knew that Bruner and me would be goin for the middle heavyweight prize, but Bruner'd won this tournament three years in a row. Hadn't even found a close match. He was known as a mean, dangerous puncher, a kid, who was now a grown man, who got his punchin practice at the Whittaker Boys Home where he grew up. I found out later that the guys from all over the state wanted to see if I was for real. They'd said to each other, "Man, if Tillis beats this dude Bruner, then he's for real."

Well, I'm tellin you, it was nothin. I didn't know nothin about Bruner; I just went out there and did my usual stuff. Yeah, Bruner was a mean puncher, but he couldn't cut me off. I'd lead him in one direction, then I'd switch and pull a southpaw move. I was fightin left- and right-handed back then. Three rounds and I kicked his ass.

"James made it look easy," Ronnie says, shakin his head. "All of the teams were in shock. Here's this guy with an impressive record and James just came in and whupped him. A man behind me leaned over and whispered in my ear, 'Man, he's the fastest kid I've ever seen around. He's only 16 years old!'"

But not everyone thought I could make it in boxing. As a seven year old, I'd been interested after I saw Cassius Clay knock out Sonny Liston. But with football, basketball, and track, boxing just hadn't come up no more. I was 15 years old when boxing came tearin after me again. My cousin Keith Reed had been livin with my family for several months before I noticed three signs hangin on the wall downstairs in the basement — "JAB," "RIGHT CROSS," "HOOK."

"What are them signs doin up there? What do they mean anyway?" I asked him one day after school, wantin to know all his business.

Bam . . . bam . . . POW, bam . . . bam . . . BOOM, he showed me in the air. I liked what I saw that day in the basement, same as I liked what I saw ten years ago on our black-and-white TV set when Cassius Clay made those fast moves. So, after basketball season, I started my boxing career at the Chamberlain Community Center on 49th and North Frankfort. It was a run-down gym in the colored section, with blocks of vinyl instead of a real gym floor and a heavy bag and a speed bag hangin from a rack. That's all I knew back then. To me, it was the greatest, a real place to train.

I still remember the guys on my boxing team: Keith "Flash" Reed, Al "Bubba" Thompson, "Sugar" Ray Johnson, Robert "Mack" McBee, DeRoss Penny, Arthur Boyd, Darrell Phoenix, Michael Zigler, Johnny Fields, Rodney Mitchell, and yours truly, James Tillis.

I came home one day after gettin on the team, and my uncle was standin there in the kitchen, so I made my big announcement.

"Hey, Junior, I'm gonna start boxing," I told him, so excited like I had ants in my pants or somethin.

"Nigger, you gonna get your head knocked off," he said, real impressed.

"Nigger," I said right back at him, "you gotta be crazy." I don't know who was crazier, Uncle Theodore "Junior" Hawkins or me, but my head and heart was in this new game and there was no turnin back.

A few days before my first tournament, my cousin and teammate Keith came runnin through the front door.

"Hey, James. You need a nickname for the paper. They're

gonna be writin about us in the paper. What d'ya want your nickname to be?"

"Well, . . . uh . . . I don't have one." I hadn't thought about this. Didn't need no nickname for football, basketball, or track. Everyone just called me Tillis or Junior.

"You got the fastest moves out there. Quick! I'm gonna call you Quick!" His dark brown eyes looked like he seen a pretty girl.

"Go ahead, put it down," I told him. The name stuck and so did my hold on boxing. I'd never let go of either.

Ed Duncan taught me everythin he knew; of course, he claimed it was everythin *I* knew. I never had the heart to tell him that most of the combinations I learned I picked up later from the greats like Angelo Dundee and Archie Moore and Harry Wilson. Ed died of a cancer in his body just this year, God rest his soul, but when I was a teenager and was just startin with boxing, he became the father that I never had. He's the one who really made me love fightin. I was hooked. Every day at school, Monday through Friday, I'd spend fifth-hour gym class jumpin rope instead of doin softball or football like the rest of my friends. One, two, three, four, all the way into the hundreds, jumpin, jumpin, breathin, breathin, for a straight 50 minutes. Man, I was gettin in good shape. Then, right when the 3 p.m. bell rang, I was out of there, runnin two and a half miles to the gym for my workout. Mr. Duncan was always there for me, ready to take me as far as I could go. But no one really thought I'd take to the boxing game so fast, not Mr. Duncan, not even my own mama.

"I used to despise boxing," Mama told a *Tulsa Tribune* reporter back in '81. "I wanted James to be in football or basketball. He was a very good football player and lettered during his sophomore year as a tight end. He was an all-around athlete.

"Then one day he came home and told me he had determined that he had a goal he wanted to reach and that was to be a fighter. I frowned about it, but said OK as long as he would do his best."

She remembered, of course, the days when I was four years old and would run into my sister's closet and pull out two tan, stitched Stacie Adams shoes. I'd stuff those pointed-toe girls' shoes, with dirt and rocks fallin out of them, on my hands, and just like my left hook was gonna change things years later in the ring with Mike Tyson, I'd change those plain, silly-lookin girl shoes into a pair of boxing gloves. I was gonna be a real boxer. I'd run around the neighborhood, jabbin shoes right and left, while the neighbors would sit there by their broken-down lawnmowers, drinkin their orange Shastas, laughin at the goofy little Tillis kid.

"What's he doin anyway?" they'd ask each other, shakin their heads at the fool playin with them shoes.

But when I grew to 173 pounds in my junior year, I guess Mama, my sisters, my 12-year-old brother, and my friends knew I was serious about somethin this time; boxing wasn't just gonna be some other sport for me or a make-believe game I'd played in the colored section of town. I told some kids once at McLain High School, "I KNOW what I'm goin to do," tryin to sound like Muhammad Ali. "I'm goin to be the heavyweight champion of the world."

"You gotta be crazy, fool," they'd say and walk off laughin.

"Hey, you guys'll just do little things if you think little. I'm thinkin big things." And I walked off with all the confidence and determination anybody could have, just like the pit bull that lived next door. One time when I saw that dog tearin into some scrawny little stray dog, almost killin it, I said to myself,

"I'm gonna be like THAT." And I was that day. Walkin down the school hallway with the Coke machines chained to the wall, empty potato chip bags and pop cans all over the floor. Just me and God and the determination of a pit bull.

That year, 1975, I won the Regional Golden Gloves in Hutchinson, Kansas, followed by a trip to Knoxville, Tennessee, for the National Golden Gloves, where I beat Paul Ramos, a kid who'd beaten Michael Dokes. The trip to Tennessee was my first time out of Oklahoma, besides Kansas, and the first time I got to ride on an airplane and everything. But the best thing about the trip to the Nationals was that I got to meet real boxers like Michael and Leon Spinks, Sugar Ray Leonard, Thomas Hearns, Greg Page, Woody Clark, John Tate, Clint Jackson, and Johnny Bumpus. All of us fightin in Nationals that year was 17 and 18 years old but the others had a lot more experience than me. They'd been trainin with guys like Ace Miller and Jim Jacobs, trainers who lived in the big cities of Chicago, Vegas, L.A., and St. Louis. But even fightin with all those big names, I ended up with the Sportsmanship Award. Just never could get real mad at anybody in the ring. My future wife, "Jane Fonda," would call it "too much heart" for a fighter.

In 1976, I was gettin ready for another National Golden Gloves in Miami, Florida, and the Olympic Trials in Vegas, but I kept gettin sick, my eyes always red and my body so weak. One day before a fight, I just ate a lettuce and tomato salad and felt good. After I beat my opponent, I thought, "Hey, this salad stuff's good for you. I'll just eat salads while I train." I didn't know that the body works off yesterday's meal and one salad after another wasn't enough to keep a 181-pound boxer goin, specially when I had to fight the 200-pounders.

Somehow I made it through the '76 Regional Golden Gloves

and won, but I was so weak. All my glitter was missin. In the National Golden Gloves at the Orange Bowl, I lost my first fight with a split decision to a boxer I'd meet again six years later in the Astrodome, Greg Page. We had no idea then that I'd be a heavyweight contender in '82 and he'd be the heavyweight champion of the world in '85. When I got back to Tulsa, I went to see Dr. Lawrence Reed, who handed me some vitamins and other stuff to get me goin. I had to get the feel again.

Dr. Reed's advice would be my first clue to nutrition, somethin a boxer really needs, but I still couldn't pull out of it to make it into the Olympics. I lost at the trials but still got to fight for the United States boxing team in Scandinavia. Thomas "The Hitman" Hearns was on our team, along with 14 others. We got to travel to places like Germany, Finland, Denmark, and Sweden, havin the time of our lives. I won both of my fights in Scandinavia, then headed home to figure out what I needed to do next.

So what does a u.s. amateur boxing champion do when he gets back from a European boxing tour? I guess a lot of guys would sit around braggin about it, but I needed some cash and I had a lot of thinkin to do. So I became a garbageman for the City of Tulsa. Didn't bother me none to get up early and pick up other people's trash. A job's a job and you just gotta do what ya gotta do sometimes. Besides, I had a lot of time to be by myself and think.

"Ed, when am I going pro?" I asked my trainer one night after a heavy workout at Chamberlain Park and a lot of thinkin in the garbage dumps. "I want to turn pro but I gotta get out of Oklahoma to get my career off the ground."

He didn't say nothin for a while.

"Tillis, I never told you this before," Ed said with this stop in his voice, like he had somethin important to tell me but didn't want to. "When you was 17, O'Grady wanted you to go pro but I turned it down. Thought it was for the best."

I didn't get mad or nothin. I knew he was right and I trusted him. At 17 I was just a young puppy. But at 19, it was time. I was a grown-up pit bull now.

Right before I turned pro, at the age of 21, when some of my friends was already comin back from vo-tech school, community college, and even big-time universities, I'd reached my all-time low. It was 1977 and I was standin in my front yard with a broken-down '57 Chevy.

Ronnie remembers that day real good. "I'd just come into town after one year of college at Central State University, and I couldn't believe what I saw. My cousin, Junior Tillis, was standing there by that old broken-down car, grease smeared all over his face and hands, wearing dirty ole clothes with holes in 'em. Here's this guy with incredible talent and dedication, who could do whatever he wanted to do, and he's just standing there scratching his head, trying to figure out who he can borrow some tools from.

"'Ricky Reed ain't gonna let me use his tools. . . . Danny Ogans won't let me touch none of his things. . . .' I heard Junior mutter under his breath, kinda in this daze or something.

"I was mad. I didn't want to see him fade away and become a nothin. 'Something's going to have to touch his blood,' I thought. And then I got an idea. I started to croon.

"'Staaaaannnnnding, wooooooonnnnnndring which way to gooooo . . .' I started singing this old Mahalia Jackson tune from back in the '60s.

"'You goin to end up not being nothin?' I yelled at him, seeing that he was already starting to get real mad.

"'Ricky Gun don't have no wrench. . . .' He was trying to ignore me.

"But I couldn't stop singing. I had to get through to him, even though I knew it was hurtin his feelings.

"'Staaaaannnnnding, wooooooonnnnndring which way to gooooo,' I kept singing to Junior, getting more and more under his skin. He was hearing me now.

"'You gotta get out of Oklahoma, Junior. You gotta make somethin of yourself,' I told him. 'Look at ya, standing there, wooonnnndring' — and then he wasn't just standing there no more. He came after me with a brick. I tore out down the street, not believin what I was seein. This grown man chasing me with a brick, tears coming down his greasy cheeks, holes in his dirty jeans, an old run-down Chevy behind him in the grown-up weeds, and he STILL had an attitude.

"'Leave me ALONE! I'm gonna kick your ass!' he hollered after me.

"But you know, the next week he left for Chicago. I was so proud of him. I guess he just needed someone to get under his skin, get him goin. And all it took was a few measures from Mahalia Jackson."

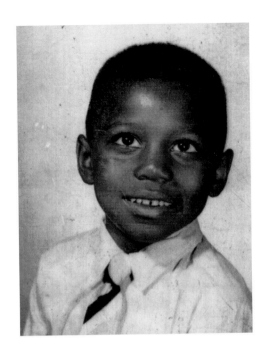

Quick — 5 years old.

Quick's Mom and Dad.

Quick — 17 years old.

Quick with Jimmy Kaulentis.

Quick after winning the Golden Gloves.

Quick with Ed Duncan.

Harry Wilson with Quick.

Quick in South Africa.

Muhammad Ali, Bundini Brown, and Quick.

Rose Tillis with Ali.

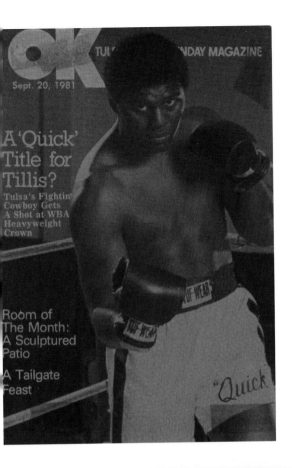

Quick in Chicago.

Quick getting ready for Weaver.

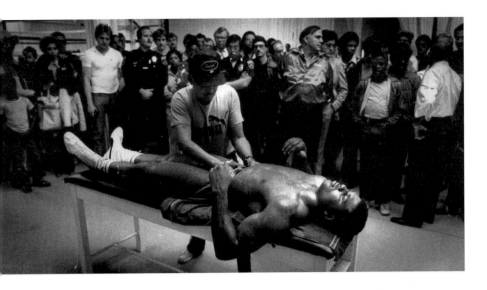

Wilson rubbing Quick down for Weaver.

Weaver with Quick.

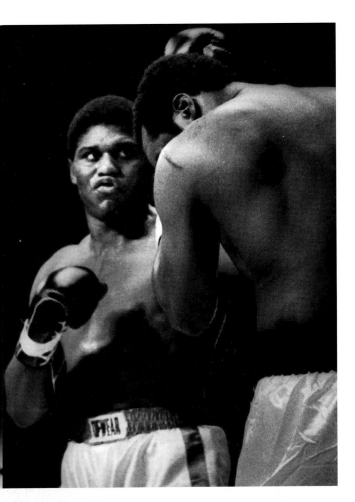

Quick fighting Al
Memphis Jones

Quick,
Archie Moore,
and Clifford Powell.

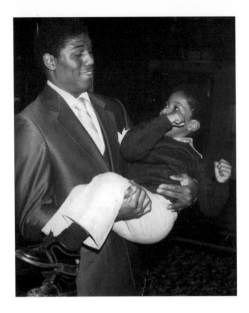

Mayo Hotel, 1979: Quick with brother
Shannon before Tulsa fight.

Heavyweight Camp 81 (with Weaver).

Quick in London.

Scene from The Color Purple (Quick on right).

Oprah and Quick on the set of The Color Purple.

Steve Young, Brenda Young, Quick, and Jane Fonda (1980).

Quick with Lenita (1991).

Quick with
daughter Icis

Iciss and Quick today.

# CHAPTER 6

# ON MY WAY
# TO PRO

The night we drove to Chicago for me to go pro, the night my nightmare ended and my dream began, my sweet little mother cooked me up a good dinner. Cornbread, candied yams, collard greens, beef stew, turnips, smothered steak, crowder peas, and lima beans. Robert and Janis Hudson were eatin dinner with us that night since they'd be drivin me there — Robert had written up a contract namin himself as my manager. He had happened to know Ernie Terrell, a famous boxer and trainer, and had discovered me one mornin when I was out runnin on Cincinnati.

Mrs. Hudson, who weighed at least 400 pounds, was hangin out by the table, eyein all the food, while Glenda and Sheryl kept makin trips, bowls piled high with soul food.

"Come awn and eat, Junior," Mama called out to me in the front yard where I was workin on my '58 Ford. Five minutes later, after I finished puttin the antifreeze in, I headed for the front porch.

". . . And bless James and the Hudsons on the road to Chicago," I heard my mama, who everyone calls Sister Tillis, tell God. Her prayer, real personal and confident, always made it sound like God Almighty was sittin there in the chair next to her. When I opened the screen door, the smell of those greens in their bowl of juice made me crazy. "Bless this food we've prepared to the nourishment of our bodies. In the precious name of Jesus . . . Amen."

"Amen!"

"Hallelujah, sister."

I passed by the kitchen on my way to the bathroom and saw that big ole bowl of greens just sittin on the table with eight people around it, waitin for me. *Mama's fixin me somethin special tonight — her baby boy's headin off for the big times in the big city.* Grinnin from ear to ear, I washed my greasy hands in the bathroom sink, starin in the mirror at one good-lookin dude, the next heavyweight champion of the world.

Plowin through the livin room, I found a spot at the table, rubbin my hands together, lickin my lips. "Mama, hand me some of those . . . greens. What happened to 'em? You gotta be kiddin me."

I couldn't believe it. An empty bowl, not even a spoonful of juice left in the bottom. I looked around the table. Mama didn't have none, Glenda had a few on her plate beside the smothered steak. *Who was this big collard-green-eatin dog anyway? Mr. Hudson? No, he didn't even like 'em.* Then I saw the crook. She was soppin up the green juice with her white Rainbow bread. Swoosh. Swoosh. "Ummmm. Ummmm, Mrs. Tillis. This sure is some good greens," I heard her say, lickin her chops like some proud alley cat who'd found a fat mouse and was just finishin it off.

Man! I'll never forget it. My last homecooked meal for a long time and my favorite dish down the drain of this 400-pound tub of lard. I had no idea what I was in for.

About midnight, when everyone in the house had gone to sleep but Mama, the Hudsons and me piled into their Electra 225, Mrs. Hudson's fat ass in the front seat with her little blue overnight bag, and me with my size-13 triple-E cowboy boots on the end of four-foot-long legs in the back seat. Between us we had five dollars, four suitcases, two boxing gloves, some boxing shorts, boxing shoes, and, I found out later, one credit card. After huggin Mama goodbye, tryin not to look into her eyes full of big raindrops, I took off for the Windy City, feelin like a giant.

We had 800 miles to go from Tulsa to Chicago, so it should have only taken 12 hours to get there, easy. But Mrs. Big Collard-Green-Eatin Hudson had to stop every 20 miles. No, not to go to the bathroom like most ladies. She had to get somethin to eat.

"Rooooooobbbbbbert, pull over to that Burger King. I need me a Whopper.

"Roooobbbbbbert, get off at that next exit and pick me up some legs and mashed potatoes at KFC. I'm gettin kinda hungry." On and on it would go, her husband just lookin at her like she was some poor starvin lady who couldn't get enough.

*Man! She's goin to eat up all the gas money.* I sat in the hot back seat, thinkin we might never make it at this rate.

When we got off to get her a Wendy's cheeseburger, large fry, large Dr. Pepper, and a Frosty, I felt better when I saw that credit card comin out of Mr. Hudson's back pocket. *Whew! Glad he's payin that bill and not me.*

Then when we got outside Bloomington I heard some cracklin and rippin goin on in the front seat. At first I thought it was just Mrs. Hudson gettin some ladies' stuff out of her bag, ya know, a Kotex or a birth control pill or somethin. But after five minutes of this cracklin and rippin, I leaned forward to see what I could see. She wasn't after no personal things, she was after her stash of candy. ButterNuts, Big Times, Slo Pokes, Black Cows, Oh Henrys, Paydays, Hersheys, Planters Peanuts,

Milk Duds, Skittles, and Nerds — all crammed into her little suitcase on top of her toothpaste and lipstick. I thought I'd die laughin, coverin my mouth and lookin out the window, anywhere besides those bags of candy.

When we got to Chicago, I saw the Sears Tower pointin up high into the windy sky, not a cloud around. "Stop here, Mr. Hudson, stop here," I jabbered on. "I gotta get me a picture of that." Out I jumped, the camera Mama loaned me in one hand, my bag in the other.

"Chicago, I'm here to conquer you, BA-BY!" I yelled in my best boomin voice, not carin about those funny looks I got. Leanin way back, aimin that camera up to the top of that sucker, I took my picture, then looked down to grab my bags. They was gone.

*Dude! What kinda place is this anyway?* I thought, gettin back into the Buick with one less bag than I'd come with. *Not gonna be like Oklahoma.*

Late that October afternoon, we checked into the Roberts Motel on 63rd and Indiana, not exactly the best part of town. They call it the Southside; I call it the colored section, the ghetto. It was right down the street from the Woodlawn Boys Club, the place that was gonna be my new trainin gym.

After we'd gotten settled in, me puttin what belongins I had left in my room, Mrs. Hudson puttin away her stash of candy, we got a call from the motel manager sayin someone was there to see us.

When I walked into the lobby, I knew things was lookin up already. A heavyweight champ of the past was standin there, waitin to meet me, a big smile runnin across his face.

"Hey," he said with this mean-soundin voice. "So YOU want to be a fighter?" It was my new promoter, Ernie Terrell himself.

"Hey, I AM a fighter. I'm full of fluid and ready to do it." A real smart-ass, ya know, talkin sweet to a past heavyweight champion who took a beatin because he refused to call Muhammad Ali by his new Islam name.

"Take this, Clay." BAM BAM. He'd gotten thrashed in the head by Ali.

"You fool, Clay." BAM BAM BAM. Another beatin by Ali. Terrell had never given in.

The next day we walked into the Woodlawn Boys Club, my new home. Ole Mrs. Hudson had been trailin behind us, checkin out all the punchin bags and half-naked black men jumpin rope.

"Hey, you Quick Tillis? I'm DeDe Armour. Your new trainer." Mr. Armour liked what he saw that day, me pullin some slick combinations, movin my feet around the ring like lightnin. I was showin my stuff; I knew I had to look good.

"He's strong," I heard Mr. Armour tell someone beside him. "Yeah, real strong." I was glad to be impressin him, a trainer of names like young Joe Louis, Spider Webb, Sugar Bear Williams, Quick Money Lumpkin.

After I finished my first workout in the PROfessionals, I was feelin high. This was where I belonged. I knew it.

"Hey, Quick. Who's that lady over there?" Armour pointed across the gym to the Big Collard-Green-Eatin Wife.

"Oh, that's my manager's wife, Janis Hudson. They brought me up to Chicago."

"Boy," he said as he leaned over to me and whispered. "I sure would like to see him get to that thang."

That same day Mr. Hudson found me a room at the YMCA on 50th and Indiana. Real fancy place, chargin thirty dollars a week. Right before he and the big one drove off in their Buick, Robert handed me exactly $30, three old ten-dollar bills.

"This will pay your first week's rent, James. Good luck to you."

"Try to just eat two meals a day," Mrs. Hudson warned me as she settled in beside her candy. "We can't afford for you to eat much."

I was standin on that corner of 50th and Indiana, didn't know nobody, had enough money to live for one week in a run-down place where the homeless live, no money for food, and no job. Hey, this was gonna to be great. *Ya know, Quick, all you'd have to do is get back in that car and go home. You don't have to stay here if you don't want to. What if you don't make it? What then? Hang out with the rest of the bums around here?*

I decided then I could conquer Chicago. Maybe I didn't have no fancy bags — hell I didn't have any bags. Maybe I only had me $30 a week to live on and two meals a day to fill my heavyweight stomach. But I had a heart as big as a giant and a God bigger than me. Nothin was gonna stop me.

But the $30 went mighty fast, and I was gettin weak without food. So Ernie started helpin me out with money to pay the rent and the telephone bill and the grocery bill. I was gettin ready for my first pro fight with Ron Stephany, only six weeks after I'd gotten to Chicago. When I kicked his ass, knockin him out in the first round, it felt good. A nice beginnin to a long string of professional wins soon to come my way. But with the purse for each fight bein only $100, I needed a better manager besides Mr. Hudson, who'd just drive up from Tulsa once in a while to watch me fight.

A few months later I left the YMCA to move into an "apartment," if you want to call it that. This one was only $65 a month, a room in an old house across the street from the Y. I found out real soon why the rent was so low.

The next mornin when I woke up to run at 5 a.m., I yanked the cord of the 60-watt light bulb hangin from the kitchen ceiling so I could see to get me some milk. The Rainbow bread sittin on the table wasn't red, white, and blue on the cover no more. It was brown — and the brown was crawlin. Fifty roaches runnin over my Rainbow bread, on the outside and in between the three pieces left inside. The place was crawlin with them.

I picked up the old-timey rotary dial phone to call my sweetheart in Tulsa, Melanie, who I nicknamed Jane Fonda. I needed some encouragement.

Onnnneeee.

Niiiinnneee.

Onnnnneeeee.

Eigggghhhhtt.

As I dialed the seventh long-rollin number, that old black dial spinnin around slower than molasses, my kitchen wall began to shake.

BOOM! BOOM! . . . BOOM! BOOM!

"Tillis, get off that phone. Don't you make no long-distance calls, you hear me?"

Ole Mr. Gasey, the landlord who didn't want no long-distance calls made in his house, could hear through those walls made out of paper and glued together with roach shit. I had to get out of there.

But every mornin, 5 a.m. sharp, I'd crawl out of the same bed the lady before me had died in, drink down a big glass of orange juice, and hit the pavement. Chicago in December ain't a nice place to be. The cold, icy wind would cut through my face, leavin icicles hangin off my nose where the snot was too cold to run. It'd be dark, with only the streetlights shinin down on the frozen drunks in their cardboard boxes. I'd be makin the final mile back to the Roach Motel through Washington Park when the prostitutes and their pimps dressed in raccoon coats would start to come out of their heated Cadillacs, callin out their wise-ass words.

"You're a bad little motherf*#!&er boy, Quick Tillis. I'm comin to see YOU fight."

"Hey, baby, give me a little piece of that good-lookin' ass. Come on, baby."

After weeks of runnin the same pimp street and winnin some fights, I started drawin me a crowd. Drunks, pimps, whores, linin the street, clappin for me, cheerin me on. "Get 'em, Quick. . . . Knock that motherf*#!&er out tonight. . . . We seen you."

Me in my maroon and gray McLain letter jacket, shadowboxing the Chicago wind, frozen snot under my nose. This wasn't what I'd been thinkin the PROfessionals was goin to be like.

It would be an angel who'd put me in the right place at the right time. The angel's name was Joe Gibson, my second father, my high-school principal, who'd become my best friend and my greatest supporter and who now sits in a wheelchair at a Tulsa nursin home with Alzheimer's, not able to feed himself. Him and his wife, Marguerite, got me a job at Shearsons, located at the Mercantile Exchange on Jackson and Canal. "Capitalism in its purest form," as Phil Flynn, a broker who works there, says.

Every day I'd have to show up in my clean white shirt, a fancy tie around my size-17 neck, my black platform shoes under my black pants — no tennis shoes or bluejeans allowed. I was called a runner and it was my job to run orders on sheets of paper that came out of the machines to the different pits where the brokers was yellin and spittin at each other.

"Five for a half! Five for a half!"

"Soooollld! SOLD!"

"Five at three! Sell five at three!"

"SOLD! SOLD!"

Numbers bein screamed out by men and women in their gold jackets and their red jackets, people with tradin-number badges and ID pictures hangin off their smocks, callin numbers out like some cattle auction before a rodeo. Insiders, runners, buyers, boys on the Merc, wheat, corn, soybeans. Chests with elbows jammin them, young, rich guys with sweaty armpits, sweat pourin off their shiny white faces.

It was before the '87 crash, the price of gold was explodin, the high rollers was bettin thousands every minute. They said you could wake up in the mornin and find out you'd made or lost $3 million in your sleep. This world wasn't for me. The pits were makin me feel the pits. All the flashin lights and all the hollerin. Them people was drivin me nuts. But, by the grace of God, my life was about to change.

"Man, I'm tired of workin and trainin at the same time. This stuff's killin me," I said in between the clangin of the bells to some man in a gold jacket standin next to me.

"What do you do?"

"I'm a fighter. I'm goin to be the next heavyweight champion of the world."

"Hmmmm . . . I see," he said, not real impressed. He looked me in the eye to see if I was puttin him on. I guess the 17-inch neck with the 187 pounds of solid muscle under it told him I might be for real. "I just MIGHT know somebody who MIGHT want to back a fighter. Let me give him a call. He's upstairs." This stranger was up to somethin.

"Hey, Jim. I got a guy down here telling me he's going to be the champion of the world. What d'ya think? Ya want to listen?"

I didn't know it at the time, but these high rollers on the

floor, the ones in the gold jackets, had the gamblin nature, always lookin for someone to back with their pork-belly money or their shiny gold. "Risk takers," they call them.

"James, uh . . . , Quick, was it? I'd like you to meet my friend, Jim Kaulentis."

I looked at this short little rascal, a little Greek guy starin up at me. *What kind of shit is this?* I laughed out loud at him, not knowin what to think.

"Ya got any money?" he asked.

"No sir. I've had a few fights but I ain't got much."

The Greek millionaire, one of two famous tradin brothers, pulled out a fat roll of money and grabbed two crisp hundred-dollar bills from between lots of their Franklin friends.

"Here, this oughta take care of you for a while," he said as he put those bills in my sweaty hand. "I'll come watch you fight and see what you can do."

I was so happy to have money in my pocket again, even my asshole was happy, jumpin out of its socket as I ran down the stairs. I couldn't even get upset when my boss fired me a few minutes later.

"Where you been? I've been looking everywhere for you! You're fired, Tillis!"

"No, I QUIT," I told him. And I walked out of that "capitalism in its purest form" place for the last time as a poor black man. Two crisp hundred-dollar bills was ridin high in my pocket.

A few days later, Mr. Kaulentis and Rory O'Shea, my soon-to-be trainer, came to the gym to see me work out. I was lookin sharp that day.

"That boy fights in a tuxedo. He's mean, but he's clean," Mr. O'Shea told his millionaire friend, meanin that I was one tough sucker but I wasn't gettin hit none.

It was my second fight, when I kayoed Al Bell in the first round, that made Jim Kaulentis see the light — the green light with dollar signs.

"Who's in for the James 'Quick' Tillis Corporation?" Kaulentis asked the mighty five.

"I'm in." Billy Lurch.

"I'm in." Bob Albert.

"I'm in." Mark Milstein.

"I'm in." Dean Kaulentis.

They all stared at the guy who'd gotten them into this.

"I'm in." Jimmy Kaulentis finished and that was that — after they each wrote out their $10,000 checks. *It was a done deal, five guys sharin my dream. They had them the next heavyweight champion of the world and they was wantin a piece of me.*

"You always goin with the white man," Mrs. Hudson told me when I flew to Tulsa for Christmas, even though her husband and her had tried to talk me out of comin home, thought I might lose my runner job.

"I'm not goin with the white man or the black man. I'm goin with the right man," I said. Her cheeks was puffin up like some bullfrog, mad as hell.

They didn't want me to go with no white man but it didn't take too much convincin. Five thousand dollars and a holy kiss. That's what I was worth. I was now in the hands of the Pillsbury Doughboy, the fat little Greek man.

With $275 every two weeks, a nice apartment at 644 West Wrightwood over by DePaul University in northside Chicago where I met my buddies Mark McGwire and Terry Bradshaw, and a food account set up at the Seminary Restaurant across the street, I felt like I'd conquered Chicago. Jim Kaulentis had become like my own father, cheerin me on at all my fights, settin me up with the best trainers, the best equipment, whatever I needed. Lots of crisp one-hundred-dollar bills in my pocket. I won 19 fights in a row, all but one in Chicago, and most of them knockouts in the first few rounds.

"James put Chicago on the map for boxing," my former trainer, Ronnie Warrior, tells people who'll listen. "Tillis was the doorway to champions. For a big guy like that, it took a lot of energy to fight the way he did. People started noticing the name and face of James 'Quick' Tillis, the Fightin Cowboy."

"Yeah, he was a real celebrity when I knew him," Phil Flynn, a Mercantile Exchange broker, says about me. "Quick Tillis was the talk of the floor, the buzzword with all the brokers after Kaulentis discovered him. He'd appear on the floor even after he quit, strutting around, looking sharp in his shirt and tie, crowds swarming around him. Kaulentis just kept him walking the floor to kind of show him off."

But it wasn't all the Chicago fights I remember the most; it was my first fight back home. Tulsa, Oklahoma — my big homecomin in December 1979. When a fighter goes home after makin it big, it's real excitin. A real big thing. The *Tulsa Tribune* and *Tulsa World* were playin it up, all the news channels were talkin about their hometown boy who'd gone to the Windy City and was now comin back to show his stuff against Al "Memphis" Jones.

I was the star of the show that night with a sell-out crowd, fans goin crazy in the Tulsa Civic Center yellin, "Quick! Quick! Quick!" over and over. But back in my dressin room, I was worried about someone else besides Al "Memphis" Jones. I was worried about Daddy. I'd ask my sister Glenda to make sure that, if he even came to the fight, he was cleaned up and sober.

"Glenda, is Daddy out there?" I asked her, pacin around my dressin room in my white trunks trimmed in red, my white robe, and my white shoes with the red tassles bumpin the air as I threw a few jabs. I was lookin like my idol, Muhammad Ali, tonight.

"Junior, I couldn't find him."

"Oh, yeah!" Man, was I relieved. My other fathers, Jim Kaulentis, Joe Gibson, Ed Duncan, they'd be there. I didn't want no embarrassment tonight. So I forgot about it. Had to get my mind on the fight anyway.

"Quick! Quick! Quick!" The crowd was gettin excited for their hometown boy.

"And in corner one, the heavyweight contender and champion of 11 professional wins in Chicago, Illinois, our own fighter from Tuuuuuulllllssssa, Oooooooooookkkkkklahoma, James 'Quick' Tillis, the Fightin Cowboy."

Just as the spotlight hit my 197-pound body and I was ready to step into the ring, I felt a hand grab mine.

"Junior! Junior!"

I turned around but I didn't even need to. I could smell the familiar breath of corn whiskey. Tulsa Drillers' baseball hat turned sideways on his head, eyes glassy and wide, dirty face covered with four days of black and gray hair, same old pee stain where he'd peed on hisself again, and some size-16 tennis shoes on his regular size-9 feet. Daddy, the drunk clown. Woooo, he was tore down.

With just a quick, disgusted look at him and his clown shoes, I dropped his hand out of mine. I couldn't mess with this stuff now. I had a fight to win, and win I sure did, Daddy and all.

*Why me, Lord? Everybody else's Daddy is made out of flesh and blood. Mine's made out of shit.*

All professional fighters have trainers — some they love like fathers, some they don't love so much. When I went to Chicago, my first trainer, Ed Duncan, who died of cancer a few months ago, God rest his soul, thought I'd deserted him.

He never could understand why I left him behind. I wanted my own people by my side, my friends from Tulsa, my supporters like Ed Duncan and Ronnie Warrior, but I also learned in Chicago all the things I didn't learn in Tulsa. And Ed Duncan had done taught me all he knew. It was my friend Archie who would start teachin me new moves I ain't ever seen. Anyhow, I didn't have much choice cuz when you get into the pros, you gotta go with who your manager says or you're out. So I went with Harry Wilson, Archie Moore, Johnny Lira, and Angelo Dundee. We had us some good times.

While fightin and buildin my record, climbin in the boxing ranks, I worked with a trainer named Harry Wilson, who me and Don King liked to call "The World's Oldest Teenager." At that time, ole Harry was 65 and his wife was 55 but Harry couldn't take it no more. He moved out of his house and moved in with a 15-year-old girl named Diane.

"It just keeps happenin. . . . Shhhhhhit," he told me one night. "I reach over to touch my wife in bed and she just grab my arm and throw it off. The other night I told her, 'I'm tired of this shit' and I moved out." Wilson couldn't say a sentence without endin it in "shit."

"My wife just wanted to make love once a month but I gotta have it every night. . . . I ain't lyin. Shhhhhhit."

If you ask me, Harry should have stayed with his wife. That Diane looked like a baby gorilla, no, an orangutan. Man, she was ugly. Sometimes after trainin we'd be walkin down the street and he'd play like he tripped.

"Whew! I thought you was Diane," he'd say as he'd be tryin to grab me all over. For two years he'd tell me, "I'm gonna go see my 15-year-old girl. Shhhhhit."

"Wilson, when's she gonna turn 16 or 17? How long she gonna stay 15?"

Boy, that nigger fell out laughin. But his jokes would make me laugh more than mine.

You see, the world's oldest teenager was born in 1917, so he was growin up durin the '30s and '40s, when Hollywood was at its greatest. The Golden Age of Hollywood, they called it. But Wilson never grew up. He was livin in the Golden Age his whole life.

Drivin down 73rd and Stony Island in Chicago (I used to think a place called island had to be some damn island) in his green '77 Chevy station wagon, Wilson would lean out the window and stare at a big ole fat black woman.

"Looky there. . . . Shhhhhit. It's Hattie McDaniel," he'd call out at her. He'd see an ugly nigger and say, "That mother-f*#!&er looks like the Phantom of the Opera. Shhhhit." He'd see a man walkin funny and say, "That motherf*#!&er walks like Groucho Marx. Shhhit." He'd see a raggly house with its windows broke out but people still livin in it and say, "Hey, that's Snuffy Smith's house. Shhhit." One day we saw two girls standin at the bus stop. "Those whores look like Amos and Andy. Shhhhhit."

He never stopped. Ole Wilson, the world's oldest teenager and the dirtiest old man I ever knew, lived more in the Golden Age of the '30s than he did in the boxing world of the '80s.

I also had two fights under another trainer, Archie Moore. Though Kaulentis was payin Archie good money to teach me the "pool table," the hook out of the corner, the pivot and jab — he'd tell me, "there ain't no soft jabs at all, boy" — Archie didn't want to spend no money on his own place. So he moved in with me and my right-hand man, Joe Kaham, at our studio apartment on Wrightwood.

I got to know Archie better than anyone wanted to know Archie. He'd talk in his sleep, first sayin "mumbo, mumbo, mummmmbo, jumbo, jummmmmbo" — at least it sounded that way to me — then he'd start in jabberin some African language, "haku miko bamsu," and he'd be fartin in between all that. One day after a heavy workout, he decided he'd do the cookin.

"Quick, you've never had my homecooked cornbread and collard greens. Let me fix you up some real good food for a change."

I heard him clankin around in the kitchen, throwin pots and pans everywhere. Just 15 minutes later I got me a whiff of somethin, and it wasn't no smell like Mama's cornbread and greens.

"What's ya got here, Archie?"

"Hot-water cornbread and fresh collard greens. Dig in."

Well, I tried but I couldn't. My knife couldn't get through those greens and the cornbread was so heavy I needed to practice liftin a few hundred-pound weights to pick it up off the plate. How was I goin to eat those things? Cuttin those greens was like cuttin through 50 rubber bands, but I didn't want to hurt his feelins none. I looked around and saw my answer. *An open window.*

Swoosh! I threw those tough greens and lead cornbread out the window by a cat in the alley and a bird on the ground.

"Man, Quick! You sure was hungry!" Moore was happier than a gopher in a pile full of dirt. "Ya want some more?"

"No, Archie. I'm real full. But thanks anyway." I smiled to myself as I looked out that window where the cat was sniffin and the bird that had been peckin at the cornbread was tryin and tryin to get off the ground. I snuck out later and got me a hamburger.

It was after Archie and me had two pro fights together that he had another great idea. "Let's go to San Diego," he told me, so excited that he looked like a little kid at Christmas. "I've got me a beauuutiful gym there and a Fleetwood Caddy. We'll work out there. You and me."

Yeah, I'd heard about his beautiful gym in San Diego and I'd heard about his house with a pool shaped like a boxing glove. But when he drove me up to that gym he'd been braggin about I couldn't believe it. An old semitrailer was sittin there with a 1966 Fleetwood Cadillac parked right beside it — not quite the gym I'd had in mind. When we went inside, I fell out laughin. He had him an old heavy bag hangin from the ceiling that looked like the bag used by Jack Johnson, the first black heavyweight champion in the early 1900s who had him a white wife. *I'm gonna be workin out on that thing?*

We went after it hard, me gettin ready for my upcomin fight with Harry Terrell. BAM. BAM. . . . BAM. BAM. BAM. I'd be hittin that heavy bag and the stuffin'd be fallin out of it. "Shea, sweep that up. Sweep it up," he'd tell Rory O'Shea. After breaks, we'd climb back in that ugly trailer, me pushin him up the steps. Bloop . . . thwoop. Ole funky Archie'd farted right on my face.

"Lord, have mercy!" was all I could say when I was messin with Archie. He was a real friend, collard greens, farts, and all.

# CHAPTER 7

# IN THE RING
# WITH CHAMPS

"We'll pay your man $1 million to step aside and let Jerry Cooney fight Mike Weaver," Cooney's manager, Dennis Rappaport, told my manager, Jimmy Kaulentis. "What do you say?"

"Let me talk to Quick. I'll get back to you."

The next day Kaulentis was on the gym floor in Miami, Florida, where I was trainin with Angelo Dundee.

"So, what do you think, Quick? Sounds like a nice sum of money for such a deal. You walk away a rich man. No fight. No pain." Kaulentis sat back in his foldin chair, sure that his money- and women-lovin fighter would bite.

But back then I was Mr. Macho Man. The only thing in my life that mattered was fightin for the championship. I'd made good money. What did I need a million bucks for when I was so close to callin myself the heavyweight champion of the world? I was young, dumb, and full of bubblegum.

"I'm goin to kick his ass," I shot back like some smart dude. "Just let me at him. I don't need no money. I need the championship title."

Kaulentis sat there for a while. "Whatever you say, Quick. I know this championship goal is part of you. If it's in your heart, then you gotta do what you gotta do."

That was my friend, Jimmy Kaulentis. A man who always respected me and understood where I was comin from. Fightin was in my blood now. It'd stolen my heart and it wasn't goin away for no million dollars.

"Fifty more sit-ups!" Jimmy Ellis, 1968 WBA heavyweight champ, yelled at me. "Move it! Move it!"

Ellis and former welterweight champion Luis Rodriguez were workin me hard at the Allen Park gym, smoothin me out, keepin my left shoulder from droppin — a habit I'd picked up when I changed from a left-handed to a right-handed boxer.

Ellis stopped just long enough to talk to a few reporters who were snoopin around. "I think Tillis will out-point Weaver. He's big, strong, and he can box. He has the speed and the endurance. If he goes the distance, Tillis will win."

Angelo Dundee wiped his oily dark hair out of his eyes. "I'm working my butt off with Tillis," he said. "We're going to win the heavyweight championship. He has natural strength and he's big all over." The greatest trainer that boxing ever saw, the guy who'd train nine champions, was excited about ME; he was about to pop, like my mama's pinto beans when she cooked 'em too long. How could I help but feel good. Real good.

"I'm goin to knock out Weaver in eight rounds!" I bragged like Ali at the press conference two days before the big fight. I was wearin my bright red T-shirt with white letters — "Believe It! Oct. 3, 1981" — spread across my chest. "I'm goin to knock out Weaver the Beaver and straighten out that jerry curl on the Beaver's head!"

Weaver sat at the other end of the table, arms folded in front of him, his face lookin like some man who'd been in the cold too long, foot tappin to my fancy words. "I'm not much for words," he finally said. "I let my gloves do the talking.

"Tillis talks a lot because he's scared and nervous. A nervous person does all the talking to try to build up his confidence. A person who knows what he's going to do will just sit back and be quiet."

Yeah, I knew Weaver was thinkin I was just tryin to act like Ali — all talk. The weird deal was, though, I didn't feel nervous at all. I was just bein me.

"Hey," I shot back. "I'm looser now than I've ever been. I'm not worried about anythin. Weaver the Beaver is the one who's uptight."

I was hearin it all from the critics. Even with my record of 20–0 with 16 KOs, some wiseguys were callin a Weaver knockout because I dropped my hands, because I'd never gone more than ten rounds, because I was straight up in the air. When you're in the spotlight like that, you just can't let 'em mess with your head. Later on in my career, though, I'd let them get to me. *Stupid.*

"The only way Weaver is going to beat Tillis is to break two of his toes," my trainer, Clifford Powell, said, a Marlboro hangin out of his mouth. "Weaver is too slow. That's the reason Thomas Hearns couldn't beat Sugar Ray Leonard. He was too fast for him. If Tillis doesn't stop him in seven or eight rounds, he will dance him to death. Like Quick says, you can't hit what you can't see."

Finally, it was the day I'd been waitin for — and would pay for — October 3, 1981. I remember seein all those cars on the Chicago streets when my trainer, my manager, and I pulled up to the Rosemont Horizon.

"Is there some kind of funeral goin on here?" I asked a pretty blonde lady who jammed a microphone in my face.

"No," she said. "They're all here to watch you and Weaver."

"Where are you from, ma'am?"

"Well, um . . . um," she stuttered, tryin to figure out why I cared about her. "I'm from Germany."

"HEIL HITLER!!" I said and saluted her with my arm up in the air. I was always crackin jokes like that when I felt good.

"Tell us about the recently formed Quick Associates who bought your contract," another reporter jumped in before the blonde could get mad at me. "How much are you getting for this fight?"

Though I'd been told it would be a $250,000 payday for my people, $100,000 in it for me, I didn't care to get into the money side of things right then.

"Quick Associates is just backin my career. They don't own me. Don't nobody own me."

"Sir, sir," the media yelled at their next target, Eddie Duncan, my Tulsa trainer, who'd come to watch the fight. "What do you have to say about tonight's fight? Is your man ready for Weaver?"

"I think Weaver's taking Tillis too lightly," Duncan said in a serious tone. "Tillis will give him a run for his money because he wants the WBA championship. If Weaver wanted to whip Tillis, he should have gone to Chicago two or three weeks ago to get used to the climate. Quick's chances are good, awfully good. The better a fighter is, the better Tillis fights. I've seen a lot of fighters show fear, but I've never seen Tillis show fear. He fears no man in the ring."

Two more of my favorite supporters came to the curb to see me, pushin all the television cameras and the flashin lights outta the way.

"Are you a friend of Quick Tillis?" one reporter asked the white couple who was holdin hands, lookin like they'd just had a new baby or somethin.

"Yes," said Marguerite Gibson, the wife of my high-school principal. "I've watched James grow up and I can tell you this.

If he knows his mother is all right, it keeps him encouraged. He feels it's his responsibility to look after her. If Quick wins the championship, it couldn't happen to a more wonderful, deserving family."

*Man, I love that woman and her husband, Joe. They're like second parents to me.* Ever since I'd walked into Mr. Gibson's office when I was a sophomore in high school and told him I wanted to meet him, we'd hit it off. He once told me that he would have been willin to adopt me as a son if I'd just asked. I nicknamed him "Pops." I watched that man and woman, who more than once filled the Tillis family refrigerator. Man, I loved them so much. Simple folks with big hearts.

"Give Tillis eight months and he'll whip Holmes," I heard Ed Duncan carry on. "Archie Moore told me Quick's got it all."

But all the jokes and braggin could not have gotten me ready for the moment I stepped through them ropes in the Rosemont Horizon ring. The scene took my breath away. Spotlights glared down at me, judgin me. My matchin red and white trunks with 'Quick' sewed on the side of my left leg started tremblin when I looked out into the audience. The whole world was watchin.

*Man, I've made it. Look at me, Mama. I've come a long way from Tulsa, Oklahoma, livin on rationed food in the colored section.*

I was pumped. Yeah, I knew I'd get tired but I thought I could get Weaver early. I was full of eggs, oatmeal, wheat toast, orange juice, baked chicken, and a few glasses of grape juice I'd snuck past my trainer that mornin. I'd trained hard with Dundee for months. I was onstage now and it was show time.

All my idols were there in the crowd of 12,000. Two rows back sat my favorite singer, James Brown, "J.B." I called him. The soul singer himself, Isaac Hayes, "The Candy Man" Sugar Ray Robinson, "The Greatest" Muhammad Ali, "Ageless"

Archie Moore, the hated Don King, "The Black Cloud" Larry Holmes, and the six-foot man who could cry like a baby but speak like a poet, Bundini Brown — all sat ringside, waitin for the action.

*Man, I love these guys. These people are my heroes. And they're here to watch ME!*

As I shadowboxed and danced around on that clean canvas where champs had fought, I saw the love of my life, my sweet mama. She was surrounded by the whole Tillis crew, minus my dad, of course. My oldest sister, Glenda, was there, as well as Olivia, Sheryl, Penny, Deah, Barry, and my little seven-year-old half brother, Shannon. The Tillises would go down in history tonight.

I'll never forget Mama lookin up at me with all her proud babies by her side, a shine in her eye that only a mother could have. I was her boy and she'd never leave my side.

*The Lord is my shepherd; I shall not want. He makes me to lie down in green pastures; He leads me beside the still waters. He restores my soul.*

The words Mama and me had just said together in my dressin room came back to me, liftin my spirits even higher.

*Yea, though I walk through the valley of the shadow of death, I will fear no evil; For You are with me; Your rod and Your staff, they comfort me.*

I'd been on my knees in her hotel room two hours before that, Mama standin over me with olive oil she'd bought at the store and then had blessed by the preacher. "Protect my son in the name of Jesus," the short, fat woman said with a voice like some African queen as she sealed the prayer with a dab of oil upon my forehead. "You can do all things through Jesus who strengthens you."

Mama always liked to pray with me and then tell me she was

"prouder than a game rooster." "You're my son," she'd say. "I gave birth to you. I knew you'd be an athlete but I never thought you'd get this far."

I threw a wink to Mama and Sugar Ray, the two idols in my life. "Mama, Sugar Ray, this fight's for you," I whispered.

*God, give me strength and clear my mind.*

Ding . . . ding . . . King Kong came out of his corner, a man just two inches taller than me, but with a huge chest and huge arms — they was ready to do some damage. We jabbed at each other in the first round. Man, I felt good, fresh as a daisy. A jab, a left hook. One, two, three, jab, cross, left hook. *This was goin to be good.* My feet were glidin faster than a bug over water, my counters quick with lefts and rights, duck, slide, fall back, spring out, feint, drop the hands. Weaver thrashin the air, tryin to land a blow.

Round after round, Weaver started to find me, hittin my face and body, goin for the kidney. Every time our bodies crashed together like the King Kong and Godzilla toys I used to play with, we'd grunt and shake, each blow enough to crack some regular dude's ribs to pieces. In round six I was stretchin out. One, two, three, four, five, six, seven. Bam. Bam. Up to 15 punches. Goin into the unknown we call it, blow after blow, never stoppin. A left hook thrown, then an overhand right. I was gettin the Holy Ghost.

Then it happened. The only fear I had, the fear even Ed Duncan didn't know about. I was gettin tired. It was my worst nightmare, like some devil's curse workin its way into my muscles, my legs, my arms, holdin me in bondage.

In the seventh round my eyes began to bug out, poppin big and wide, ready to be snipped outta my skull. I couldn't find enough air. Gaspin for every puff I could find, I started feelin this deep burn in my chest. *No air. No air.* I tried to breathe deep like Dundee had taught me but I couldn't find air. My chest felt like fire, each breath like my throat had red-hot lava poured down it. My butthole kept openin and closin, my body lookin for air from somewhere.

But I was too proud to stop.

"I should have taken the money," I remember thinkin as I staggered around lookin for the head I needed to hurt. Like they say, a bird in the hand is worth a million in the bush. I'd thought I had that Weaver bird in my hand, I'd thought *baby, I got this one in the bank.* But he was goin to be one tough sucker.

I fell into the corner as Dundee stood over me, wipin me down, talkin me up.

"Who do you think you are, Quick? You want to be a bum all your life?" he yelled at me, knowin those words were what I needed right then.

Suddenly I felt a gentle touch on my ankle and I recognized that warm, powerful hand.

"Junior, you can do it. I just know you can," Mama said.

I looked over where the Tillises sat. My sisters weren't holdin their heads up high no more — they was prayin with their heads down, their eyes shut tight. *It's killin them.*

Though I was dead tired, somehow I found enough strength to hurt Weaver bad in the 13th round when I switched to a southpaw stance and hit him with a straight right jab. THOMP! A big wail from the crowd sent chills down my black and blue body. They tell me I was staggerin around somewhere between consciousness and unconsciousness, tryin to keep from hittin the floor, but Weaver held on, refusin to fall. I couldn't put him away. *Too tired, too tired.*

I lost a 15-round split decision that night, goin into no-man's-land. That's what they call it in the boxing game, like when Muhammad Ali and Joe Frazier went 14 rounds. When a fighter goes more than 12, like 13, 14, 15 rounds, he's pushin into no-man's-land. It's mighty tough and the fight will be close but after the 12th round it's whoever wants the fight the most. I knew I'd won 11 rounds but all I walked away with was $100,000 — of which Uncle Sam enjoyed $40,000, of course. Yeah, I'd end up with $60,000 and a broken heart.

A fighter hates to go to his dressin room with a loss and I was ashamed that night. I'd disappointed all my idols — Sugar Ray, Ali, Holmes, Mama.

A knock at the door made me jump.

"Come in," I heard a hoarse voice crack out of my throat.

"Son, you know you won that fight, don't you?" my mother asked in her quiet but sure way.

"Yeah, Mama, I know. But tell the judges that."

Another knock at the door, this time a lot harder and louder.

"Come in . . ."

A 215-pound black man with fuzzy sideburns stickin out below his fro and a silly mustache hangin above his lip smiled at me through the doorway.

"God bless you, James 'Quick' Tillis," Weaver said. "You're a good fighter."

The champ's words meant a lot to me that night. I knew I'd given him a run for his money, all $700,000 of his purse. But I was broken by that damn demon's curse, tiredness, and by that shame of losin in front of my idols. It would take a while to get it all back again. I didn't know it then but it would only be nine months before the toughest fight of my career was gonna happen. It'd be a fight that would take two and a half years out of my life, the fight with Earnie Shavers.

I kept tellin Jane Fonda to quit messin with me.

"You need to quit sending your mother all that money," she

would say. "You've got to take care of yourself."

"Just shut up about it," I'd reply. "I gotta get ready for this fight. Don't be messin with my mind. Get away from me." I loved her a lot but I couldn't allow her to mess with me at this important time.

"Well, she's not your responsibility. Your money is my money," she said and she walked away.

I called Melanie, my first wife, Jane Fonda because she was always talkin about how she wanted to be a movie star or maybe a famous lady like Diana Ross or Lena Horne. We'd gotten married in April 1980, five months before the Weaver fight, but the marriage only lasted four months.

Though my first marriage with her was finished, my love for her wasn't. I couldn't get her off my mind. My manager, Kaulentis, decided then that no matter how much I loved that woman or how much I wanted to get back with her, there was no way he was lettin her in the doors of the Tillis–Shavers fight. Kaulentis refused to get her a ticket. She'd caused me enough headaches in the Weaver fight. Even though she wasn't there, she'd been on my mind and Kaulentis wasn't goin to let it happen again.

I'd seen Earnie Shavers fight Muhammad Ali, the fight that many say started Ali's sickness. I'd seen him go after Larry Holmes, causin Holmes to stagger like a drunk. Man, that boy was one tough dude. No doubt about it, Earnie Shavers should go down in history as the toughest and the hardest-hittin man in boxing records. Never before and never again did I experience such killer hits.

I walked into Las Vegas's boxing mecca, Caesar's Palace, on June 19, 1982, at 5:30 p.m., durin most people's dinnertime. It wasn't gonna be no feast for me, though; I was bein thrown to the lions for a little snack. For the first time, I was scared. I knew this one wasn't gonna be easy. I just wanted to get out of the den alive.

Harry Wilson and Angelo Dundee had been trainin me for this fight so they were both in the corner with me. My right-hand men, one handin out my water, another one wipin me off and cuttin me if I needed it. I could tell they was nervous, too. This was gonna be one mean fight.

The bell rang. I started throwin punches at his big, black, bald head, like a jackhammer comin down on his concrete skull. Usin all the combinations in the book. I had him on the ropes. Jab, cross, left hook. Right cross, left hook, the unknown. And then he got me good — an overhand right. *Man!* My right leg shot out from under me.

*DAMN, that hurt!*

Ding!

The first round over, I walked slow back to the corner where my trainers was waitin for me. *I gotta think about this again.*

I came back at him for three more rounds, takin every chance I could get to send punches his way, aimin for that crystal-ball head of his. Our bodies banged against each other, sweat and snot flyin everywhere, attackers circlin, feintin, tryin to land mean punches where they counted. It was workin.

*No problem . . . I've got him . . . I can do this.* After the fourth-round bell sounded, while walkin back toward my stool, it happened.

No one saw it comin, not Dundee, not the World's Oldest Teenager, not even Jesse Jackson or Bill Cosby, who was starin us down from the audience.

Bam! I felt a sudden blow to my jaw. *That SOB.* Shavers had come around me as I had my back to him and knocked me hard from the side. My gloves were down, I was feelin real cocky, and Shavers had seen his chance.

"Man, Wilson, maybe this nigger shot me shit," I yelled at my trainer who was yellin at the referee. "What kind of shit is this?"

The man in the crooked bow tie and wrinkled white shirt and black pants screamed at Shavers, "Who do you think you are pulling something like that? I won't have that in my ring!" Meanwhile Wilson settled down and started workin on me, his champ. Starin up at me, knees bent, the little 5'5" man with all his 145 pounds started to do his job. He was determined to keep my focus on the fight so he ignored Shavers' illegal hit. Like a father sendin his son off to war, Wilson gave me some last-minute advice. "Quick! Quick! Keep your hands up! Keep your back off of the ropes!"

At the sound of the fifth-round bell, I started to grab for the enemy but felt some kind of tug on my leg. "Quick. Keep your ass off of the floor," Wilson told me one last time.

I don't get mad, really mad, too many times, but Shavers' big-assed trick had me goin. So I went right out there and outboxed him. Outboxed him easy. Round six, seven, eight. Spinnin him round, hittin him when I wanted to, throwin punches at him like a kid smackin a watermelon with a baseball bat. KA-POW! KA-POW!

It was round nine when Shavers got me by surprise again. Like boxers say, it's always the punch you never see comin that causes the most problems. Kind of like the "phantom punch" of the second Ali–Liston fight.

I saw him comin at me. It was that big, bald head of his that I remember, zoomin in at me like some missile findin its target, ready to strike. I just stood there lookin at this bald head, then BAM! An overhand right smacked me square on the chin. Boom! I was down like a sack of flour. My friend Ronnie Warrior remembers it too — "he landed on his knees then fell forward like the giant from 'Jack and the Beanstalk,' arms outstretched, all in slow motion, a bellybuster without any water."

I'll never forget the effect that hit took on me. I'd walked into the Land of Make-Believe. Some fighters hear harps playin, some see the Day of Judgment or just plain darkness. For me, it was saxophones and trombones soundin in my ear with one low-pitched note. *Eeeeeeeeeeeeeeeeee*, all one note, like a bagpiper who fell over dead with no one to stop the last note. As the note rang in my ear, I saw little blue rats scamper out to smoke cigarettes and eat Spam sandwiches.

"One! Two! Three!" The referee knocked me back into the real world, a world of pain I didn't really want to be in.

"Four! Five!" Cosby and Jackson watched, all disappointed, as they started to grab their drinks and move out of the crowd. Sugar Ray Leonard sat there feelin sorry for me, one boxer to another — he'd learn later what it felt like to be on the floor. Another manager, Willy B, who I hadn't met yet but who'd later ruin my career, stood in the shadows.

"This guy's a goner," I could read on all their faces. They were sure they'd seen the last Quick Tillis fight.

It was then that I looked straight out at Eddie Taylor, AKA "young Joe Louis." Half of my face was flattened against the slimy ring, the other half feelin good. With my one good eye, I winked at Joe, my stablemate, my friend.

"Six! Seven! Ei — ."

The referee stopped right in the middle of his count. He'd seen miracles happen before, but nothin like what he saw then. I shot straight up, a goofy smile on my face. Yep, old Quick had risen from the dead. God hadn't let me forget that He was my Shepherd. I could fear no evil for He was with me.

The next thing the commentator, Howard Cosell, knew, Tillis and Shavers was back at it again. I tried to find Shavers but all I could see was three of those big bald heads. I remembered, right at that second, Archie Moore's words — *hit the one in the middle* — so I grabbed the middle head. Lucky for me, it was the right one.

The crowd didn't know it that night, but they was not just gonna see a fight and a resurrection that night; now they was gonna see some real fancy dancin. Two heavyweights, 427 pounds put together, started to dance. We do-si-doed, we did the two-step, the Charleston, and the Tennessee waltz all over that bloody floor until I could get my head together.

I somehow got through that ninth round, but it was gonna be the tenth round that'd put Shavers away. Noticin that Shaver's legs were givin out, Dundee told me to hit him with a one-two and push, then another one-two, push. Yep, this trick, like so many of Dundee's tricks, worked. That dude could hit so hard that he could bring back tomorrow and still turn goat's piss into gasoline — but I won the round.

"Six–Tillis. Four–Shavers," rang out one judge's score. "Seven–Tillis. Three–Shavers," another one. "Seven–Tillis. Three–Shavers," the final judge announced to the crowd.

*Sweet. Sweet.* But I'd never been so tired in my life. I'd beaten the hardest hitter ever but I was exhausted, nothin left inside me to even enjoy the crowd goin nuts. All I knew was I'd made that concrete face of Shavers' hurt; he'd been cut open bad, a four-inch bloody gash where his left eyebrow used to be. Me? Just a bad, bad headache.

All used up, fallin on the dressin room chair, I heard a knock at the door.

A man the whole world knew strutted in with his big fat cigar, ashes hangin on the end, and found a chair. "Quick," the voice said kinda sarcastic like, "you got to do better than this."

I looked at Bill Cosby, not believin my ears. Who was he to

come in here with such words after what I'd been through?

"Nigger," I said. "What fight was you lookin at? Did you see me get up off of the floor and KICK HIS ASS?"

I was tired and hurt. You know, you just don't talk to fighters like that when they've gone to hell and back. What did he know about takin hits in the head that could've knocked my brains out? I knew all about it, and I didn't like smart talk like that.

I found Jane Fonda that night waitin for me outside Caesar's Palace, angry that she couldn't get into the fight. But it just took one look at her winnin man to change her mood.

Back at the hotel, Melanie wanted to make love to her champ. But you know, man, when you can't, you can't and it was one of those nights. I was too tired for her lovin but not too tired to borrow some words from my friend Rudy Ray Moore.

> *Baby! I couldn't come over there if you called me.*
> *I'm tired of candy and I'm tired of cake.*
> *He hit me on the chin and I'm too tired to shake.*
> *I'm tired of cookies and I'm tired of gum.*
> *If I couldn't get another piece now, I'd feel real dumb.*
> *I looked at her through my tired eyes, smilin and happy.*
> *I'm tired of prosperity and I'm tired of luck.*
> *If it was another cherry to get, I'd be too tired to duck.*
> *Baby, I'm ti . . .*

But before I could finish, I closed my eyes to see the land of blue rats, cigarettes, and Spam.

The next fight of champions kinda happened by mistake. I was scheduled to fight "Terrible" Tim Witherspoon on Don King's card at Stouffers in Cleveland, Ohio, on September 10, 1982, but I was told the fight had been called off. Witherspoon's manager wanted more money.

Ya know, I never did drugs, never drank booze, never smoked, but the one bad habit that messed with me time and time again was my foolin around with women. I guess it's all those looks you get from dolls that drive a fighter like me crazy.

So instead of turnin in early that night, I ran around Cleveland chasin the prettiest girls I could find. Jane Fonda and me hadn't lasted too long with our first marriage and the ladies were linin up. "Whooo," I'd say with my flirtiest look, "first time I've ever been knocked out without a punch." "Whooo," I'd coo to another, "you could catch fish without a hook. You moooove me." Quick, quick, quick. Sure enough, when I came breezin back to the hotel at 5 a.m., the World's Oldest Teenager was there to greet me.

"Quick, a new fight's on, same day and place as Witherspoon. Stead of him, you'll be fighting a guy named Pinklon Thomas," he said.

"Never heard of him," I shrugged. "I'll take 'im out in two rounds."

Later that day, Kaulentis came into my hotel room with some advice. "Quick, you better be ready for this guy. I'm warning you."

"Yeah, yeah." I was ready for this one.

Three days later I learned. Thomas' first jab busted my lip. Man! I couldn't get goin for nothin. Round after round I gasped for air, not knowin what was causin the problem. I should have put Thomas away easy that night, but he was more up for the fight than me. I hadn't taken the fight serious and I'd pay for my cocky attitude. And it wouldn't be till four years later, right before the Tyson fight, that I'd learn what was causin the tiredness that kept me from goin the distance with so many fighters.

Thomas TKOed me in the eighth round that night. I felt so

bad about that loss I went out and got married for the second time. That's how it worked for me — when I felt down on myself, I'd go and do somethin crazy to build myself back up. Her name was Gail Davis, a beauty I'd met in Chicago when I was trainin for Page and she was collectin money for kids with cerebral palsy. Except my love for Jane Fonda had never left. I couldn't quit thinkin about her durin trainin, durin meals, durin fights, durin sleep. My head and my feelins were messin with me and would soon cause the only father I really looked up to, Jim Kaulentis, to leave me.

I'd fought a guy named Greg Page in the 1976 National Golden Gloves at the Orange Bowl. Though I liked him as a person, I admit I hated him as a fighter. He'd beaten me on a split decision so I was wantin to fight him again. Lucky for me, my next fight was scheduled with him for October 15, 1982, in the Houston Astrodome.

But it was like God wouldn't allow me to get past a first round without a bloody lip. BAM! His fisted glove slashed through my flesh like a lion tearin apart his only meal. I was mad now. Jab, right, one-two. Jab, right, cross, left hook. BAP! BAP! "Stick him! Stick mean!" someone from the crowd yelled, lovin every bloody minute.

Page fell on his knees after that combination in the second round. Ding! The second round was over but my anger wasn't. Before I knew it, I ran over to that punk and WHAM! WHAM! I whacked him with a hard left hook, right in the head — an out-and-out foul. The referee chewed out my ass for that stupid move and gave Page 15 minutes to pull himself together. But once again, like in the Shavers fight, my chest burned with a pain that ate through my body. I had the focus in my head, but I didn't have no strength left in my muscles to finish him. My arms felt like a wet, twisted rag, my legs like a dyin quarter horse goin down. Page countered me with a right lead and I was done for. He finished me with a TKO in the eighth.

Somehow I managed four straight victories after that, bringin me to a 1983 bout with Tim Witherspoon for the vacant North American Boxing Federation title. Critics would later say that I was "easily distracted by outside influences that kept me from concentrating on boxing at hand," that I'd slipped into "the journeyman circuit." They were right. I only made it one round before Witherspoon knocked me out.

I'd divorced Gail a year earlier, so it wasn't that, but still my mind was never on the fight. It was in Oklahoma with my ex-wife Jane Fonda, still crazy about her. That night Fonda told me she'd fallen for another guy, who ended up bein some kinda con man, and a few months later, my manager, Jimmy Kaulentis, left me for good. The Witherspoon fight convinced him that my mind wasn't in the game no more. "Jimmy, I don't want to see you get hurt," he told me on his way out.

My "outside influences" were probly different than other athletes' problems — it wasn't cocaine, marijuana, steroids, or Jack Daniels for me. It was somethin called bein down, angry, and missin my woman. I'd let flyin words like "you don't have a chance" get under my skin and ride me until I'd told myself that maybe a black kid who'd gotten Ds and Fs in school, who'd lived off USDA cheese and lima beans, who'd grown up embarrassed by his daddy's drinkin, really had dreamed too high. So instead of usin that anger to help me, I'd look for the prettiest woman I could find to make me feel good again. I've learned from those mistakes.

After my Chicago lawyer, Jeffrey D. Jacobs, who claims "the D is for dependable," landed me a bit part in a movie, *The Color Purple*, with Oprah Winfrey, Danny Glover, and

Whoopi Goldberg, my manager and me decided the fun had to stop. In July of 1985, after my parts in the movie were filmed, we headed south to Willy Lock's Gym in Johannesburg, South Africa, where I'd train for two months to get ready for Gerrie Coetzee, the 1983 WBA heavyweight champ. Coetzee had lost an earlier fight to Greg Page with a KO in eight rounds, but had knocked out Mike Dokes (who beat Mike Weaver in a world title fight that ended in a record 63 seconds) in ten rounds for the WBA championship title. I would take home $16,000 and learn later that my new man, Willy B, would steal $100,000 under the table for himself.

All I remember about that night was the stingin punches I gave and got, the closed-fisted jabs, the left hooks, the one-twos, one-twos, and the serious damage I did to Coetzee. Fist and glove were talkin that hot night in Johannesburg. The referee finally called the fight after the tenth round, me losin to a split decision. With calls of *Booooo* ringin through Ellis Park, the medics carried the bloody champ straight to the hospital. I'd cut his right eye so bad that it looked like one big piece of raw steak, closed shut by the swollen eyelid; the gash in his lip wasn't lookin no better. They told me later that I'd loosened a few teeth of the fighter who'd been a dental technician before steppin in a ring. But though I walked real easy through the black and white crowd to my dressin room with not even a scratch on me, I felt low. I just couldn't seem to win the ones that counted.

I'd reached the place where Floyd Patterson had been 20 years before me, wantin to find a door in the floor that would open, fall through it, and never face the crowds again. It's a good thing I didn't give up, though, because my luck was gettin ready to turn. They'd call him the "most awesome heavyweight since George Foreman," "one of the most effective machines of pure destruction ever unleashed." He was the one who'd knock Marvis Frazier flat in 30 seconds. But I'd be the first man to go as many as ten rounds with one of the toughest fighters ever — he had a string of 19 KOs, and only three other fighters had stayed on their feet with him. Mike Tyson was about to meet his match.

# CHAPTER 8

# TIRED,
# SO TIRED

I started throwin up mucus. That's what finally made me get in the car in February 1986 with Jane Fonda, who I'd married again, and head to some backwoods place on Admiral Street called Earl's Health Food. What was waitin inside for me was gonna change not just my life but the boxing history books too, both for me and for Mike Tyson.

Melanie, my Jane Fonda, nagged me for seven years to go see Earl, the owner of Earl's Health Food since 1958. I found out later that Earl'd been told he was dyin with prostate cancer in the early '50s, got a kidney taken outta him that didn't need to be, then was sent home by a medical doctor who smelled like booze at the time of surgery: they'd given Earl two weeks at the most. But durin five years of bed rest and lookin into nutrition, Earl cured himself. He'd grown up on those pioneer things like horsetail and cayenne herbs, squirrel broth, and coal oil for medicine, which had kept him alive as a young boy after bein kicked in the chest by a horse. He learned that the doctors' medicines sometimes just looked to make people worse.

But Earl and me seemed to have somethin in common, even though I'd never met him. The determination that would keep him healthy — he's 83 today — is the same determination that would keep me from givin in to this tiredness, a tiredness that was suffocatin me after five rounds. I was to fight Mike Tyson in three months and I wasn't worth nothin. In Reno, South Africa, and Lancaster, Pennsylvania, Marvis Frazier, Gerrie Coetzee, and Tyrell Biggs had gotten me good, either in the eighth or tenth rounds, because of that burnin in my chest and no air gettin to my lungs. I needed nutrition help from my trainer, but he didn't know jack. Each day before trainin I'd eat stuff that I thought'd bring me energy — ya know, stuff that's supposed to be good for you. Lots of milk, eggs, cereal, orange juice, Uncle Ben's rice, cream of wheat, cheap hamburger meat, pork chops, Rainbow bread, and some 7-Up or Hawaiian Punch sometimes, and maybe a bowl of ice cream after a tough match.

"Come on in," said a kind, young-lookin lady with blonde hair down to her shoulders. She pointed us into a tiny office that'd been a kitchen where her sweet mama had baked home-made millet and whole-wheat bread to sell, gettin up at 3 a.m. after her 12-hour waitress shift to sweat in the kitchen. "My name's Conni. I'm Earl's daughter and I run the store now. I'll be the one who will give you a consultation today."

*I don't know who she thinks SHE is, but I'll hear her out . . . see what she's got to say.*

"My name's Quick Tillis. I'm gonna be fightin Mike Tyson in May and I need some help. I ain't got no wind anymore and I don't know what's wrong."

"Yeah, right, sure you are," Conni later told me she'd thought to herself, lookin at this big black man she'd never heard of who didn't seem to have enough energy to even block a punch from her.

"I don't know anything about boxing," she told me as she sat on an old wooden stool with piles of books everywhere, words like "nutrition" and "healthy eating" written all over them.

"But let me take a look at you."

And with that, this kind-lookin stranger with glasses gently picked up my right wrist and placed her thumb on it.

"How much pop do you drink?" She had this wise but weird look in her eye, like she knew everythin bout me from a few pulse beats.

"Well, uh, uh . . ." How'd she know that little secret? "Ya know, a little in between fights."

With my right hand still between her fingers, she slid her hand down to my fingernails like she was gonna read my yellow nails instead of my palms, like I'd heard some weirdos do in the back of houses with beads hangin down over the doors.

"Your circulation's slow. Stick out your tongue."

"Yes, ma'am," I obeyed. She had my attention now.

Instead of one of those tongue depressors I seen doctors use, Conni pulled out a black flashlight from her desk drawer and quickly started shinin it all over my tongue and around my throat.

"Aaaaagggggghhhhh," I gagged, tryin to ask her what she was up to, but before I could she'd pulled down my lower lip and was checkin it out.

"How much bread have you been eating?"

"Well, you know, I have bologna, sometimes peanut butter sandwiches and stuff like that for lunch, buns with my hotdogs, potato chips, corn chips." I didn't see no problem with that. Protein and all.

"You have a serious mineral deficiency," she said, feelin my ring finger. "You also have low energy, your pulse is too low for what it should be."

*No shit. I been knowin that all along. No energy, no nothin.*

"Your adrenalines are weak and you have a vitamin B deficiency." She stared at my eyes and tongue.

"What are you seein in my eyes, anyway?" I joked with her. "You readin my eyes or somethin? You're not goin to put no spell on me or nothin are you?"

Not a laugh, not even a chuckle. Just a small smile, sure of herself.

"You've got a prostate irritation from all that pop you drink, James. You also have too much active yeast from all those sandwiches and jugs of milk."

Whoa. Now she really had my attention.

"Ma'am, what'd you say? Did you say prosTRATE? Don't that have somethin to do with your sex organ?"

"ProsTATE. Yes, it can." She was gettin kinda red now.

"Ma'am, I'll tell you right now, there ain't nothin wrong with THAT." Me, always jokin. Jane Fonda and Conni looked like they didn't get the joke.

"James, get serious." Jane punched me in my big tired shoulder. "Do you want to hear what this woman has to say or not?"

"Well, what does all this mean anyway, ma'am? You say I don't have enough of these adrenaline things and I got too much of this yeast stuff. What does it mean? Why am I so tired all the time? That's all I wanna know. You gotta help me get my strength back." I was at a dead end.

Conni cleared her throat, pulled out a sharpened pencil from her top desk drawer along with some paper that had columns of lines on it, and started writin. I think she saw the panic in my eyes.

"I'm going to put you on a strict diet of certain foods and supplements. If you want to feel better, you must follow these directions. Are we clear?"

"Give it to me."

"You'll start your day with two tablets of liver concentrate, two tablets of drenathyphin for adrenalines, one capful of Body

Toddy for liquid minerals, 28 drops of Total B, three tablets of Promotal, a derivative of wheat-germ oil for energy, two tablets of Enzamatic Digest for better digestion, one teaspoon of Nutra-Vite powder for multiple vitamins and minerals, two tablets of All-C-Plex for vitamin C, two tablets of Pantathenic Acid for more vitamin B, and one tablet of Beta Carotene for oxygen."

I sat there with my mouth hangin open, that mucus backin up in my throat again. She had to be kiddin me. But the look on her face told me she was dead serious.

"What else is for breakfast, baby?"

She smiled this time, gettin used to my friendly way. "Eggs, millet toast, applesauce or some other fruit but NO melons."

"You sure eggs are OK with all those ways they can screw up your heart? What about those egg things you can buy without the yolks?"

"Mr. Tillis, if God wanted that egg yolk and that egg white separated, He would have done it Himself," she said. "Don't worry about that."

She kept on with her serious look. "Now, you are allowed a mid-morning snack — one protein drink OR a handful of raw nuts, almonds, pecans, walnuts, cashews, anything but peanuts. Then, for lunch and supper, repeat the same formula I gave you earlier with the same number of tablets and drops. You may have one vegetable from under the ground and two from on top with a lean meat — "

"Under and on top?" I interrupted, laughin as I thought of my Grandpa Theodore under 300 pounds of Grandma Olivia, makin love, shakin the whole house.

"Yes," she said, never skippin a beat. "For example, carrots and turnips grow under the ground, lettuce and zucchini squash grow on top. Now, for your protein, you need lots of good, lean red meat such as — "

I couldn't help it. I had to interrupt again. "You mean you aren't one of those VEGeTARians?"

"No, a person in your career needs all the meat you can get, but no more hot dogs or bologna; those are the leftover parts from things that you don't want to know about. Calf's liver, roast, steak, and fish that aren't shellfish or scavengers: cod, salmon, trout, bass, halibut. Those will work fine."

"You're killin me here, Miss Conni," I said. "I don't know if I can do all this. What am I supposed to drink to wash all this cow liver down anyways?"

"All the milk you're drinking is what's going to kill you, Mr. Tillis. All the wheat and dairy products you're consuming are causing that mucus to back up into your body; the wheat and dairy products convert to sugar, which then ferments in the colon and backs up into your body — an overload of mucus, you could say.

"Your adrenalines have 52 purposes and one of those purposes is to provide your body with concentration and energy. I'm going to send some dandelion herbal tea home with you and I want you to also drink papaya juice and black cherry juice. No more 7-Ups or orange juice. Drink lots of water, along with those juices, three to five times a day."

Forty-five minutes later, I was only $100 lighter and 11 bottles heavier. But I was too weak and too desperate to fight the voice in the back of my fuzzy brain. *You gotta be crazy takin all this stuff. What the hell. I'll give it a try. Anyways, nothin from nothin leaves nothin.*

Draggin myself out of bed the next day, I swallowed my 15 tablets, drank my gallons of liquids until I thought I'd puke, ate my fancy millet bread from the toaster, and went out the door, dreadin my daily run in Riverside Park. I had no idea what was about to happen — it'd be a run, all right. A whole different meanin of that word.

Thwump. Thwump. Thwump. My cheap runnin shoes hit the dirt trail. The mornin sun hadn't come up yet. It was just 5 a.m., so there was no early mornin traffic yet, just blackness and the cold March air huggin me like my mama used to do when I got home from school. It took me a while to notice but I was feelin better already or maybe it was just me hopin. No, my wind seemed to be longer. The mucus wasn't comin up my throat either. Thwump, thwump, thwump, thwump. Faster and faster, smoother and smoother. Then it happened. All that stuff Conni had given me started to do its trick. It was time for some SOUL cleansin. UGH! I could feel it happenin, workin all that crap out of my body, cleanin me out. It was like a whole new body was bein made, a butterfly crawlin out of his cocoon gettin rid of all that junk hangin on. *Man, I need to find a bathroom before those wings start comin out.*

No such luck. *No way, man!* I panicked, my stomach bulgin like a big ole king snake eatin his dinner. I had to go REAL BAD and it was gonna have to happen NOW.

I headed for the bushes, arms huggin my belly. And then it came. The runs. Over and over and over again. Heavin and gaspin until I didn't think nothin was left inside. Thank the good Lord there wasn't one single walker or jogger that mornin at 5:30 to get a good look at a 230-pound man crouched over in the tall weeds, the sun startin to shine on one big black ass. Yeah, all that old stuff, my old ways — ice cream, soda pop, milk, bologna sandwiches, hot dogs — it was history now.

Baby, I sure felt good after that. I'd been a fool not knowin nothin, and my manager Willy B not knowin a thing either or at least not lettin on that he did. I'd never be the same again. It was out with the old and in with the Quick.

I had seven weeks to get ready for "the little GOrilla" — that's what I like to call him. My new manager, Willy B (his name's been changed, of course, to protect his guilty ass) brought in some big names for sparrin, like Leroy Murphy, cruiserweight champion, and Mike, AKA Tank, Brown. I'd never felt so good about a fight in my life. Drew "Bundini" Brown's words still were goin through my mind. "Champ, God gave me something to give you," he'd said before my fight with Marvis Frazier in Reno.

"Nigger, what is it?" I'd asked.

> *You don't float like a butterfly and sting like a bee*
> *Cause you ain't Ali.*
> *You're the fightin cowboy.*
> *You ride 'em, rope 'em*
> *Brand 'em and corral 'em.*
> *You the fightin cowboy,*
> *Old dude.*

I really was floatin like a bee.

May 3, 1986, came and it was gonna be me or him. I hoped, with my new Earl's soul-cleansin routine, it'd be me.

I stepped into the ring, shadowboxin a little, feelin fresh, my white cotton robe showin the title "James Fighting Cowboy Tillis" against the bright blue canvas ring (I later dropped the 'g' in Fighting). The ABC audience read the stats on me and Tyson: 19-year-old Tyson, 28-year-old Tillis; 5′11″ Tyson, 6′1³/₄″ Tillis; 215-pound Tyson, 207-pound Tillis; 70″ reach Tyson, 76″ reach Tillis. "Here comes Mike Tyson lookin like some kind of warrior or gladiator," remarked one of the commentators. Tyson was wearin some silly hairdo on the top of his head like he'd been shaved with a bowl over his head, a thick mat of hair on top.

The bell sounded. Round one. I thought I'd come to wrestle a loose bull at an Oklahoma rodeo the way Tyson charged at me out of his corner. WHAM! The little GOrilla was in a hell of a rage, like he'd been smokin weed and just found out I'd killed his mother or somethin. If I hadn't moved when I did, the Tyson–Tillis fight would have been over before it even started. I started my dance, makin lateral movements around him, circlin to the left to keep the gorilla off balance. I was on his ass and he knew this wasn't gonna be the easy ride he'd hoped for, not like his other 19 opponents.

Tyson couldn't get set for nothin. I was stiff-armin him like a tackle in football, Tyson tryin to get inside, usin an overhand right, clenchin, tryin hooks that wouldn't land. I was showin HIM how to fight. "I can't believe it," said one commentator. "Tyson is clearly disappointed at how his left hooks aren't landing. Tillis seems to be getting Mike Tyson out of his game plan."

I was amazed. The first few rounds were nothin for me. Them calf's livers and millet bread was kickin in. Tyson moved like a slug, guardin himself, throwin a few double jabs, but I kept scorin with right uppercuts. It was Tyson who was wearin down.

"Well, Jim, I'd call the first round even and possibly give round two and three to Tyson, but he doesn't appear to be very aggressive tonight. Tillis seems to be taming Tyson. The Cowboy can punch when he's fresh, can't he?"

Near the end of the third round, we got into a hell of an exchange. My hands were tyin him up but Tyson didn't want to take no chances. "Boooooooooo!!!" The crowd hadn't expected this; they'd come to see a KO but their champ wasn't deliverin. Tyson landed a left hook but I was all there. I backed him against the ropes, a first for Tyson. We closed with a flurry, fists flyin through the air like a thousand bees comin down to sting.

Fourth round. Lungin at Tyson with a left hook, I suddenly

felt air and not his ugly face. Too late. He rolled up under the punch I'd wanted him to feel and caught me with a mean left hook of his own. Boom! I went down fast on my ass then bounced right up again.

Durin the second round, he had tried my trick and took a fast-movin lunge at me. But when he tried it this time I was ready for him, slipped the punch, and hit him with a hard blow right in the stomach of steel. Bloop!

We both heard this poof of air go off between us. "Quick, I farted," the champ gasped in my ear.

"Oh, that's all right, Mike," I answered. "I mostly make 'em shit."

And in the fifth round I almost did. I couldn't believe it — I was still fresh, knockin Tyson all over the place. *Hey, I don't believe this!*

Round seven, I was still fresh. *Lord have mercy!*

Round eight. *Good God Almighty! I'm kickin his ass!*

Round nine. *Lord Jesus. I'm fresh as a daisy!*

Round ten, the round that had been costin my fights, the round that always took me out. *I can't believe this. I'm fresh as the mornin dew! Thank you, sweet Conni.* The world was seein a new Tillis and they didn't know why. As one reporter wrote that day, I was "holding my own with one of the most devastating fighters of all time," a man whose future 35–0 record would include 31 knockouts. But I wasn't goin to be one of them.

"Tyson isn't doing his job in punches, Jim. . . . Tillis is looking rather fresh. This is NOT a good round for Tyson. He's letting isolated punches go and is NOT using combinations." The commentators weren't real sure how this fight would finish but they were pullin for Tyson. After all, people was expectin the GOrilla to be the next Ali.

Ding! End of the tenth. I couldn't help it. He'd gotten me mad and before he knew what hit him, I came around Tyson and smacked him in the jaw with a right hand. The writin was on the wall of Tyson's hometown of Glens Falls, New York, and José Cortez, the referee, saw his chance to stop the fight. I knew I'd beaten him fair, but how could a fighter like me who was tryin to come up the ladder beat a champ like this, a champ who had the million dollar bets sittin on him?

Staggerin toward each other before the decision was announced, Mike held on to me, just as sure about his loss as I was about my win.

"You beat me, you beat me," he swore under his stinky breath so that only I could hear him. "I'll give you a remath . . . a remath," he lisped in his high little voice, gaspin in between words, tryin to find air in the ring.

"And the decision iiiiiiiiiiisssssssss," the announcer's voice rang out. "Six rounds to four, Mike Tyson. . . . Six rounds to four, Mike Tyson." And then the final judge's card came up for everybody to see.

"Seven rounds to three, Mike Tyson!"

"Booooooooooooo," the crowd of 7,600 New Yorkers in Tyson's own backyard yelled, not believin the decision.

Reporters swarmed everywhere; man, they loved these controversial decisions.

"So, what do you think, Quick?" they asked me when I was makin my way to the dressin room. "Do you think you should have won?"

They kept after me. "How does it feel to be the 20th loss to Tyson?"

"I beat that boy," I yelled at the cameras. "I'm gonna fight him again. He's a good fighter. I ain't puttin him down, but I beat that boy."

Knowin about Tyson's rape trial comin up in Indianapolis, how he'd hurt his woman, I had to add, "I'll get Tyson next time, if he don't go to jail first!"

I got my chance one year later, but not in the way I wanted. I stepped into the ring with the little GOrilla for a four-round charity exhibition in Chicago, sendin him to the ropes 11 times. Later I sparred with Tyson before he fought Tyrell Biggs. But while Michael Spinks became a multimillionaire for gettin kayoed by Tyson in 91 seconds, I made just $12,000 for goin 10 strong rounds with him (and I had to give $6,000 to my manager, Gary Bentley). Yeah, the reporters would later say, "Tillis, a proven warhorse who has been in the ring with seven men who have held the heavyweight championship, has the distinction of being Tyson's most troublesome opponent, going a total of 14 rounds against him." It was a day of glory for me, the mean ole warhorse, but not a big payday for the fightin cowboy from Oklahoma.

"When you go to pay the bills," I told the reporters, "they don't ask how many rounds you went with Tyson. They ask if you got any dead presidents. You know, Jackson, Grant, Washington — those pictures on those dollar bills."

It's just too bad Tyson's opponents, like me, wasn't paid by the minute. If they had been, me, and not Michael Spinks, would be the one countin dead presidents today.

# CHAPTER 9

# IT'S A
# DIRTY GAME

"For every one fighter that promoters are building, four to five fighters are takin the fall. That's the business." Yeah, that's what my boxing friend Ronnie Warrior told me years ago, but I didn't wanna hear it. I got taken — big time — and one dirty promoter cost me my career. I ain't mad now, I'm just a little smarter.

It had all started with a flight from Los Angeles to Tulsa and a turkey sandwich, two years before the Tyson fight. But I wouldn't find out about no dirt till two years later, after my big fight with a guy you might have heard of — Evander Holyfield.

"This kid's a black kid but he can fight. Very profitable. If we do things right, this kid will make you a million bucks in a very short time. He's black . . . but he's damn marketable." Pat O'Grady, the guy who wanted to be my manager after Kaulentis, was dyin with cancer in his body, so he was tryin to sell me to Willy B over a turkey sandwich in an Oklahoma City fast-food joint one day in '84.

Willy B took the bait. "Yeah? That good, huh?"

"I'm tellin ya, Tillis is a hot commodity. I'll give 'im to ya for $300. Just send me the money to show me you appreciate me."

"I'll do it. I'll do it. Give 'im to me."

Sold! I'd been sold for $300. Three hundred bucks that

O'Grady would never see, but two million bucks that Willy B would pocket after usin me. Man, it's a dirty game.

Lorenzo Boyd, my boxing friend who's still fightin in the ring today and would choose to die in the ring before dyin in a car wreck, reminds me it's always been that way. Dirty.

"Tillis, our game came from the slums of England. When it got to the u.s., the mob picked it up. Back in the old days, the guys who ran boxing were jus some hardcore thugs; today the thugs make a lot of money, tearin up casinos. Boxing's an underworld sport. Them guys sell you out . . . someone's always on the make."

Ronnie Warrior agrees. "You try to tell me that the Mafia doesn't control sports when a basketball player makes $20 million. The Mafia is full of smart people. They can't do it like they used to in the '50s and '60s, so today they get well educated, form industries, get 'em some clean-cut guys, put some guy as president of an industry on paper, and bingo — they're in.

"The Mafia will always control boxing. They told Sonny to get out in the first round, so Sonny got out in the first round. When ya owe 'em, your life is on the line. And Sonny owed 'em."

"Yeah, it's organized crime all right," Lorenzo agrees. "They make their bets behind the scene. I call it the long money versus the short money. Tillis won that fight against Tyson, no question. But Tyson had the long money; it was his hometown and the bets were on him. Tillis had the short money. If he'd been given the decision, that fight woulda changed his life, Tillis could have had another title shot. But he got the short money. It's such a hokey business.

"What's a fighter gonna do when $30,000 shows up in his account? Fighters can't be bought so easily now but there's still 100 roads to that ring.

"When you're rich, you call these guys in the Mafia and the

crooks who call themselves promoters, ya call 'em 'eccentric.' But when you're from the ghetto like me and Tillis, you call 'em 'hokey,' 'kinky,' 'kooky.' It's a helluva game."

Yeah, you gotta watch your back and your bank account, but I didn't know nothin. You see, when ya fight, your head's gotta be in the game. You don't have no time to be messin with who's doin ya right and who's doin ya wrong, who's stealin what and how they messin with you. My friends tried to warn me. Jane Fonda tried to tell me but I couldn't listen then — had to focus, had to keep my head in the game. Nothin else. That's how they get you.

I'm smarter now but it's too late. If you're in boxing, jus watch your back. Don't trust nobody for nothin.

At first, I trusted Willy B. I thought he was gonna be jus like another father to me. Like Ed Duncan. Like Joe Gibson. Like Jim Kaulentis. I was always lookin for that father I never had, hopin to find one in my next promoter. After all, Willy was gettin me some good fights, like Frank Bruno, Mike Williams, Gary Mason, Gerrie Coetzee, Joe Bugner, and Mike Tyson. I didn't need no fancy place to stay or fancy equipment. Jus three good meals a day, a place to train, a place to sleep. Back then I wasn't thinkin much about money, makin millions. I just had my mind on one thing — gettin to the top, winnin the title. And Willy B knew it.

He started with cuttin the trainin expenses down to nothin. The way it works, a promoter is sent money for the costs of a fighter's trainin — gym use, sparrin partners, food, sleepin arrangements, transportation. I found out later that Willy B would charge $20,000 for trainin expenses for a fight worth $45,000, but he made damn sure them trainin expenses would be as cheap as he could go.

Ronnie, who was managin other fighters then, worked close

with Willy B and saw most of his dirty moves.

"B would tell the sparring partners he'd give them $500 a week for sparring with James; then, after the week was over, he'd end up giving them $250. James didn't know for the longest time what was goin on. B would cheat me out of the money he owed me, sending me $5,000 when he'd promised $10,000. When he got cash, he'd take $5,000 off the top for himself, pay out some to James, the least amount to the others he could get by with, then pocket the rest of it."

Lorenzo got pulled into the dirty game too. He came to help me get ready for Tyson in '86 at the Red Shield Boys Club and never got paid a dime.

"Tillis was a big-time fighter back then and I was a nobody. I was in his camp with big names like Alfonzo Ratliff, Leroy Murphy, the cruiserweight champion, and then there was little nobody me. Tillis was in such good shape, just spanking the crap outta me. Lows here and lows there. He had five weeks left to get ready for Tyson and all his big-time buddies had left. They didn't want to take a beatin to help Tillis get ready. So I got the job."

He laughs about those weeks. "I was the only body left for Tillis to whoop up on. Yeah, I was young and strong so I'd go to the ring every day to take my whoopin. We'd have us a good workout . . . at least I did. Six rounds a day for five weeks. Willy B never paid me a thing for all that."

I can forget the diamond necklace and the weddin ring that Willy B stole from my first and third wife, Jane Fonda, and the super-8 projector he stole from me and the way he bragged to Ronnie about how he was sendin his twin boys to private school and college and the Mercedes and the new house he bought — all from pimpin me — but I can't forget the way he set me up in the Holyfield fight. I can forgive him cuz I can't hate nobody or hold no grudge against nobody, but I can't ever forget it. He coulda killed me.

Ronnie heard the conversation when Willy B was in his downtown Wagoner hotel room on Highway 51 before the Holyfield fight had been set.

"I was coming up the steps to give B a few more details about the upcoming fight," says Ronnie, "when I heard him on the phone with someone. I didn't think much about it because promoters are always on the phone, but it was what I heard that made me stop in my tracks.

"'He ain't gonna beat him. Guaranteed . . . he ain't got no legs no more.'

"I started easing up the steps then. Had to make sure he didn't hear me coming. QT was my friend and I needed to hear what B was doing to him.

"'Yeah . . . yeah. No . . . I'm sure of it. Yeah . . . the altitude. Yeah, he needs more days to train in high altitude. Yeah . . . I'll be sure to take him up there just a few days before the fight. . . . Yeah, I promise you, he won't be ready. See you in a few weeks. Bye.' There was this click and the TV came back on. I stood there not believing what I'd just heard. All I could think was that I had to go alert James. This news could save his life, just in time. So I got out of there fast.

"I found James gettin ready for his early bedtime. 8 p.m. sharp. By 8:01 he'd be sleeping like a baby. Never a care, never a worry. But I had to tell my friend.

"'James, James, get up! You need to know what Willy B's doin to ya,' I said, 'You gotta hear this. LOOK AT ME!'

"'Ronnie, I got me a fight in a few weeks. Gotta get my beauty sleep. Go away.'

"'TILLIS! He's settin you up. Willy B's settin you up. He's making sure you won't be ready,' I tried to warn him.

"But my brother wouldn't listen. 'Oh man, I don't wanna hear it. I gotta be focused. All that money puts me on edge, Ronnie, ya know that. Go away now, let me get some sleep.'

"I thought I'd slipped out away from B real quiet but I guess not. Either that or he'd needed to check in on James one more time. But he heard us talking. He was on to me like I was on to him. And the next morning he told me about it.

"'HEY you, RONNIE,' he yelled at me the next day, motioning me over to him while we were working James in the gym. 'Whatever you heard last night, don't be bringing that up again. You HEAR me?'

"'HEY, that's my FRIEND out there,' I told him, knowing that I had to stand up to him sometime. Might as well be now. 'What happens if his lungs collapse in that altitude and he dies up there? What THEN? HUH? HUH?' I was really mad but he wouldn't pay me no attention. He had more important things to attend to.

"Hey, LOOK, Warrior, if you go messin this up for me I'll knock Tillis's brother out of a ticket. You know Barry needs to be there for spirit. He's Tillis's inspiration. You gonna take that away from 'im? You mess this up and neither you OR Barry gets a ticket up to Tahoe.'"

James be nimble, James be Quick. James jumped onto the Holyfield pick. The phone woke Willy B from his sleep this time.

"Holyfield and Tillis both want a bite out of Tyson," said the voice on the other end of the line. "How about July 16, 1988, at Caesar's Tahoe, Stateline, Nevada? Your boy and mine. What d'ya say?"

Before I knew it, I was trainin for the fight of my life with Evander Holyfield, the undefeated cruiserweight champion of the world, who wanted to show his heavyweight power against me. I'd be ready for him.

On the night Tyson pounded Michael Spinks in the first round at the Atlantic City Convention Center, me, the only boxer ever to come close to beatin the heavyweight champ, was sound asleep at a small house near Wagoner, Oklahoma, more than 1,200 miles from the bright lights of the ringside. I had to get my sleep. When I train, like Ronnie said, I'm in bed by 8 p.m. so I can get up early the next mornin and run. Even though I was pullin for Mike, I had my own fight to worry about. I was on a mission.

This one was gonna take some serious trainin and I only had two months to get ready. I weighed 228 and needed to trim down to fight my enemy — Holyfield had dominated the 185-pound class since he'd won the bronze at the 1984 Olympic Games. A lot of my friends in boxing do a bunch of liftin. Not me. I don't lift weights to build my strength. Liftin makes me too tight and my fast jabs gotta be loose, all the way from my head to my toes. Loose, slip and slide. I guess if Herschel Walker and me can keep up our muscles like we do without the weights, who needs 'em? You got to go at trainin slooooowwwww and eeeeaasssy. You got to cook the cake by addin one ingredient at a time. Like my friend Archie Moore told me, "You have to build a man like you would a house. Block by block, not just thrown up. Everything has to be done step by step."

I started by usin all the Archie Moore and Bundini Brown tricks. I'd loosen up with jumpin jacks, windmills, ten minutes on the jump rope, shakin my shoulders. Next came the axe. Woodchoppin. First, five slow chops. My manager and trainer Willy B kept bringin the wood out. Five chops. Ten chops. By the end of my trainin, I'd be up to 100 chops. Then came the shadowboxin while I pictured Holyfield right in front of me. The little black beauty cruiserweight comin at me and I'd shadowbox him for four rounds, jab, jab, in and out, in and out.

Then I'd work the floor. My friend Bundini Brown had taught me to never train the same way day after day. So Monday, Wednesday, and Friday I might hit the heavy bag for three rounds with a one-minute rest between. I'd go back and forth with the speed bag for ten minutes straight, some days the jab bag for three rounds. Other days I'd jump rope for four to ten minutes, followed by some crunches and rockin chairs to tighten my stomach. Then I'd work up to sparrin with the toughest partners I could find, always changin the routine so I wouldn't get burned out. "Can't get stale," Bundini would tell me. He'd compare trainin to sex. "Ya gotta work up to it easy. Don't get spent too early. Keep the hard-on in training and come in the fight. Ya don't wanna come too early."

I had to be disciplined all the time. No eatin junk food or drinkin sugary pop, like Conni had taught me. No lovemakin. No socializin. Run early, eat right, train right, be strong, mentally and physically. Two months later, I'd done it. I weighed in at 210, lean and mean, like George Foreman's grillin machine. Finally, I knew I was ready.

"Tillis, Tillis, do you actually think you can walk away with this one?" The press was really hot that night. "Will this be your break against Tyson? Will you show Holyfield what it's like to be in the heavyweight class?"

"I'm goin to initiate him all right," I countered. "And when I'm through, I think Tyson will be givin me another shot. Holyfield's given me a shot to make some money and get another shot at Tyson. He picked the wrong somebody."

"How did you drop your weight?" yelled someone from behind me.

"I've been trainin hard and I'm in the best shape of my life. Even Ray Charles could see that."

Then the reporters laid eyes on the Holyfield gang drivin up to the curb.

Holyfield's solid black body stepped out of the limo, his face lookin like it had been carved like some Roman statue.

"So, are you going to be ready for Tyson after this?"

"If I don't beat Tillis," he replied, "there ain't gonna be no Tyson."

Dan Duva, Holyfield's manager, had a few words of his own. "Tillis is a good fighter. Sometimes he looks good, sometimes he looks bad. He's capable of one hell of a fight. We're hoping he doesn't have that kind of a night."

I decided to play a little. "Movement," I said. "That's the key. You got to slip and slide, style and profile. That's the key to this Holly Angel. Evander Angelo. Evangelo Angellio. Whatever his name is. I told him he sure got a pretty name. I call him Mildred." The crowd broke out laughin. *I'm enjoyin this moment.*

The crowd of 5,000 was ready to see some action. When the first bell rang, the future champion came at me with a bundle of energy. We threw punches at each other and the crowd roared in delight. In the second round, Holyfield jolted me with a right-left to my head, forcin me into his corner. But when the bell sounded, I wasn't finished. I fired back more punches to his head. BAM! BAM! The crowd loved it — the more illegal it got, the better. But Duva didn't care for how I was treatin his man, crowd-pleasin or not. He charged up into the ring, madly grabbin for my gloved fists, tryin to handcuff me, fists behind my back.

"Break it up! Break it up!" he shouted at me, face turnin all red.

Man, it's not a good idea for some sissy manager to come up and try to get in a fighter's way — especially when the fighter's throwin illegal punches at his opponent. Madder than one of them bulls at a rodeo, I turned on him, ready to fight anyone who got in my way. The cornermen poured into the ring, loosenin one of the ropes from Holyfield's corner. Whoosh, whoosh, whoosh. Ropes flyin, managers and trainers, fighter and fighter shovin and yellin, lungin at each other, grabbin sweaty arms and oily chests. It looked like a night of professional wrestlin — Stone Cold and Hulk Hogan in the boxing ring.

Willy B eventually got me calmed down, rubbin me down in my corner while I kept eyein the Roman statue in the other corner. But somethin was wrong with me. No matter how deep I breathed, openin my mouth and nostrils as wide as I could, I couldn't get no air. *Oxygen, oxygen. Someone get me oxygen.*

I'd find out later that I'd been set up. Ronnie had tried to warn me about Willy B's plan but I hadn't listened. Bad move.

It wasn't gonna be the curse of tiredness that'd wrap itself around my leg and arm muscles this time; it'd be somethin else that I'd had no experience with and, unlucky for me, I'd learn about it the hard way. It was called altitude. I was just a country boy who felt most comfortable in a old leather saddle gallopin through the wavin wheat of Oklahoma's plains. I didn't know nothin about a 6,360-foot altitude that could rip out all the oxygen in your body, leavin you dizzy and nauseated. I'd been trainin in cowtown Gibson Station, Oklahoma, altitude of 674 feet.

It was the fifth round that did me in. Holyfield went for the head, sendin me flyin against the ropes. BOOM! BOOM! KAPOW! Right uppercut. Left to the head. My neck flew back, stars swirled around my eyes. As my head flew forward again, another glove came at me, a red blur of glove, a rocket comin at my face. Amazin how fast a fist can move, just a split second, and I was havin trouble dodgin the blows. Couldn't breathe. Like the Weaver fight but this time it was the altitude. *Air . . . air. I couldn't make it. Can't fight with no air. No wind.*

Once he got me on the ropes, it was all over. Though I was shakin, not able to help it, sweat pourin off my chest like a man dyin of a heart attack, I was determined not to go down. Ding! Somehow I'd managed to stay on my feet but I was gonna say words I never thought I'd hear myself say.

"I quit . . . quit. . . . Stop," I heard myself spit out, blood and spit sprayin on everybody around me. I wasn't a quitter but ya gotta have air to fight and I had nothin. Sittin on my stool with my head bowed, a dead-tired loser, I was sorta aware of the referee, Richard Steele, by my side.

"Get Dr. Dehne. Quick don't look good. Now! Now!"

The fight was called. I'd survived five rounds with Evander Holyfield, but to me, the altitude and Willy B was the winners that night. I walked away with $20,000. B bought himself a house and enrolled his son in a private school with his earnins — $200,000.

"You didn't have no choice," Ronnie reminds me. "The fight went on, you survived five killer rounds with Holyfield, but the 6,400-foot altitude did ya in. You never had no air. No chance. I'm just glad ya lived to tell about it, James. You're my friend and I'm glad he didn't kill you up there. But it's no thanks to Willy B."

A fair take for fighters is 70 percent, 30 percent for the promoter. I was told that Holyfield got around $100,000 for our fight that night; I got $20,000 and Willy B took 15 percent of my take, plus $300,000 to $400,000 under the table doin "business." For the Tyson fight before that, Tyson got $200,000; I ended up with $12,000 after B's take. Before Tyson,

I was told that B got $40,000 for the fight with Carl "The Truth" Williams in Atlantic City, and I got about $2,000.

Man, it's a dirty game, ain't it?

It was the whitin out of contracts that really crawls under my skin though. That's how he did it, that dirty crook Willy B. Ronnie learned about it later.

"Yeah, when B learned that I was on to him, after the Holyfield thing, he stopped getting me fights," Ronnie says. "He wanted to pay me peanuts for fighting Frank Tate, who'd won the gold medal, said he'd pay me $1,000 and throw in $200 on top of that. I did the fight only cuz I needed the money back then, but I never saw it. I found out later the fight was worth a lot more than that. B pocketed the money for himself, and sent me home with an airplane ticket that used up almost $1,000. Never saw that extra $200 he promised me. But then that's the way he worked. Using you to get all the money he could for himself.

"I found out how he was crookin James and me. He'd get the original contract, get James to sign it, then white out the original amount and type in the amount he wanted. Tillis was signing duplicate forms with B whiting out their shares, then giving himself more, James less. I'm sure B did this to a lot of his fighters. He really messed with 'em. There ain't no way B would ever resurface in England or Atlantic City or Oklahoma today. Those British promoters would literally kill him if they saw his face. Same thing in Oklahoma and who knows how many more states."

Lorenzo Boyd caught him once but didn't really want to go into it with me over the phone.

"I was green and didn't know nothin," he says. "But one night it all came together and I discovered 'one incident.' I kept a better eye on things after that. [Willy B] was like they say King is, that he could get you more money but the rumor was that he was stealin half of it. I didn't see nothin he stole from me with King, but when I caught him stealin he knew I knew.

"Funny thing is, though, that I didn't play his game. He wanted me to get all over him but I threw him cuz I stayed cool. Ya see, B fancies himself a tough guy and if I had gone combative, then he would have just gotten more upset. But I didn't want to play it that way. When I came out of my room knowin what I knew, I just looked at him in the eye and said, 'Let's go eat.' I thought, 'What would he expect me to do?' and I knew it wasn't that. He told me later, 'Well, son' — he tried to call me 'pretty boy' but I never let him peg me with that name — 'I just needed the money,' he told me. That's all that was ever said and I looked for another promoter after that."

Lorenzo's gotten smarter too. He's had to learn how to lie right along with 'em all. He told me that when trainers come up and ask him how he's doin — "You been trainin?" they'll wanna know — he's learned to lie to 'em. "Naw, I'm afraid not," he'll tell 'em, "I been eatin burgers, spendin time with my wife. Been doin nothin, man. Just sittin around gettin fat."

One guy he thought was his friend called Boyd to see if he was in good shape for a fight. He thought his friend was behind him, backin him, but he was just checkin for the opponent's manager. Doin some spyin on his own friend.

"Man, it's a dirty game, Lorenzo. Why you still in it?" I asked him.

"I figure I know the whole game by now. I know the dirt and I still love it. I'm kinda fascinated by it all. Tillis, I'm in this club you big guys were in . . . I just snuck in the back door. I know the whole game now and if anythin happens to me, it's shame on me."

"Boyd, you'd die for this game, wouldn't ya?"

"Ya dang right I'd die for it. You were a top world-class fighter, Tillis. You were at that level because you loved it. That's what drives me now, too. I love it, man — just like you did."

"Every promoter has a little of Don King in him," Ronnie tells me. He's right. Hey, I love DK. He's one smart nigger and he don't care if I say that either. If you can fight and you got heart and you're with King, you can make some money. Sure, DK juggles fighters. He signs with two fighters, buildin 'em both to the big payday, but he's not gonna lose. No way. DK ain't comin home with empty pockets.

Everyone in the business makes it look like King is the only dirty one but he's not. He gets singled out cuz, as Ronnie says, "an African American isn't supposed to have as much control as he does." Ronnie wags his head back and forth, back and forth. "No, King, he's assertive and persistent, that's what HE is. He beat 'em at their own game, so they call him dirty."

DK is big time. Hey, a million dollars ain't nothin for King, but a nigger — African American, like Ronnie calls him — ain't supposed to have the kind of money he has. I love DK. Willy B's white, Don King's black. So what? Ya got dirty people in all races but King knows how to treat his fighters right. If DK ended up makin $60 million off Larry Holmes and Holmes walked away with only $10 million, hey, how can a fighter be mad at somebody like that? Other promoters like Bob Arum, Cedrick Kushner, Butch Lewis, Goosen Brothers — they're all in the same business with big-time money. None of these big-time promoters got time to steal nickels and dimes from their fighters like Willy B. The real promoters pay you what they say they're gonna pay. They might make big money under the table, too, but the difference is that they'll pay the fighters big money, not keep it all for themselves. Big promoters don't even like to mess with small-time dirt like Willy B. They don't got time for his kind.

It was when I was sparrin with Tyson so he could get ready for Carl "The Truth" Williams (Tyson'd knock him out in the first round) that DK gave Ronnie and me $500 each just for some spendin money. Man! I hate sparrin cuz I like to be the boss but when DK handed us some extra spendin money, it was our dream. It's every fighter's dream. He took us out to eat dinner with him one night, and the next mornin for breakfast he was eatin with Ronnie's opponent. Sounds crooked but that's the business. DK will treat ya right, though, none of this pimpin stuff.

"King told me after the Pinklon Thomas fight that Tillis was the best heavyweight out there," Ronnie tells me after all these years. "King told me one time, 'I got all respect for Quick Tillis. I'm not worried about Larry Holmes — it's James Quick Tillis everyone should worry about. He's the closest thing to Ali I've ever seen. Thomas won because I caught him at a good time when he'd been out all night.'" Ronnie said King smiled at him with that smile of his, his black and gray hair stickin out all over his head. "'Yeah,' King said, 'I caught 'im on a bad night.'"

I had some good fights on King's card — Thomas, Shavers, Page, Witherspoon — but I let DK down. My body was either gettin too tired or my head was screwed up with them crazy women. DK will do his fighters right though if they work hard for him, but I can't say that much for the nickel-and-dime managers like Willy B.

I thought my luck was turnin in '91. I'd just gotten back from an exhibition match with Larry Holmes in Jakarta, Indonesia, when I met a guy named Abe Hurshler.

"Willy B's cheatin me, Abe," I told him when B wasn't around. "What am I gonna do?"

Ole Abe had 'im the name of another manager or two that he thought would be good. I like to call 'em Amos and Andy. So Abe set me up with 'em, gave me some spendin money, and things was lookin good again.

My next fight was gonna be in Atlantic City with Tommy "Gun" Morrison. He would take the '95 WBO Championship title from George Foreman but a year later he'd hear the awful news — medical suspension for HIV. Today the poor guy's fightin the disease and tryin to get outta jail for carryin guns and drugs.

The first thing I noticed that didn't look so right with the Morrison fight was that Andy bought him a fancy house in Virginia where I was trainin. Me? I didn't have no food, no car, and the apartment where I was stayin got locked up one night cuz Amos and Andy hadn't been payin the rent. My friend and hairdresser Kenny Lucas got me through by buyin me food, lettin me stay with him, givin me a car.

"Man, Kenny. They're stealin me blind. I ain't got nothin and they buyin them fancy houses. I can't believe this is hap-penin to me again. Just like Willy B."

"So get rid of them, James. Why do you put up with this anyway?"

"What am I supposed to do? I'm here trainin for Morrison, I gotta pay child support to that crazy woman. Man, I gotta be cool, can't go jumpin on 'em or nothin."

The day before the fight my good friend and backer Abe came checkin on me. "Hey, Tillis, you makin out OK?"

"You kiddin, Abe? I ain't got nothin. My friend Kenny's been feedin me and stuff. I thought you was gonna send me some spendin money to live on."

"Hell, Tillis, what d'ya mean? I've been sending you money every week . . . about $18,000 by now. How can you be hurtin?"

"Those $%&#@ pimps. I knew it, stealin me blind."

"What are you telling me, Tillis? You haven't seen none of it?"

"Nah, you kiddin? It's history. I'm tired of messin with the dirt. I ain't gonna do it no more. I'm done."

Man, Abe was mad, but probly not as sick down deep in the gut like I was. I decided then that I couldn't trust nobody for nothin. I'd give 'em their show but I wasn't gonna put nothin into it — and, you know, I was the guy who was used to givin all his opponents 10 to 15 rounds, so that wasn't like me. I ain't a quitter, but I had to have a payback and the Morrison fight was gonna be it. One round was all they was gettin outta me tomorrow night.

I hated it. It still makes me sick to think about throwin a fight cuz I'd never done nothin like that before and I never would again, but I couldn't let 'em crook me — not this time. Eighteen thousand dollars I was supposed to be gettin and I never saw a dime, just like with Lorenzo and Willy B. I had to do it and it wasn't hard. I like Morrison and I don't have nothin against him, but he couldn't even punch, he couldn't whoop me in a million years. But I let him have the fight when I went down in the first round. Had to make it look good so I let him punch me then went down after three knockdowns.

"Yeah, I watched James train," Kenny says. "James's experience and knowledge of the game looked excellent when he was training in Virginia. Then when I saw the fight, I noticed James was taking punches but not delivering any — that wasn't like the Tillis I'd seen. He didn't make the fight look fake or nothin but I can tell you, Morrison didn't really beat anyone in that fight. He hadn't really fought anyone up till then so Tillis really just gave Morrison another notch in his belt . . . just helped him out."

Crazy things happen and it seems like every time I start to get somewhere, somethin even crazier happens. I thought Willy B was outta the picture, but he called the cops on me that night. Abe hadn't let him in on the Morrison fight cuz Abe liked to use his own people, so B saw his chance. He knew I owed some child support money so he threw the Atlantic City cops a juicy black bone. Me.

After the two-minute fight, they came and got me. It was a helluva night, throwin my only fight ever, gettin pimped by pimp number 1, pimp number 2, and pimp number 3, then gettin arrested and thrown in jail. The police chief let me out after I paid $3,000 — about half of my earnins from the fight — and I washed my feet of all the dirt, but I can't ever get it all off. Them feet are as stained as hell.

I found out the hard way. I got took by a crook. And if I had to do it all over again, I'd fight even harder, but I'd watch my back next time and listen to my friends who was tryin to save my career and my life. Talk to my boxing buddies and my wife about it. And don't trust nobody. Yeah, Ronnie said that for every one fighter the promoters are buildin four or five are takin the fall, and I guess I was one of them four or five he was talkin about — I took the fall. All 220 pounds of me came tumblin down, with Willy B's and Amos and Andy's rich little asses tumblin right after.

# CHAPTER 10

# THE MOANS AND GROANS OF WOMEN

Like I've said, it was the crooks who got me — but somethin else blinded me, too. It was them damn women.

"When I first laid eyes on that young man, I knew he was a real specimen of a man. That chocolate skin, dark as the deepest, darkest Hershey bar. And when I saw for the first time the body under that robe of his in the boxing ring . . . honey, I knew I was in for trouble."

That's Jane Fonda for ya, always a way with words. I was 19 and she was 20. It was 1 a.m. at Disco 3600 on Cincinnati and 36th Street and "Sweet Thing" by Chaka Khan was playin real nice like in the background.

When I asked her to dance with me, my heart stopped.

"Baby, I liiiiike you. Mmmmm, mmmmm. You moooove me."

"Hey, you're too big for me to move YOU."

"Baaaaaabbbbbyyy, you mooooove my HEART."

She was wearin a blue cowl-neck sweater and some tight jeans. I got her address and phone number before the dance was even over. I was in love.

But Jane, Melanie Hughes, didn't know what she'd gotten herself into. The life of a fighter wasn't gonna be a smooth road. I was just gettin ready to turn pro but didn't really have no direction at the time, and she was in the middle of goin to college at Central State University. Still, that didn't stop us none.

Me in my red '57 Chevy with them high-rise airplane seats and her in the dorm, we'd get together on weekends and have us a good ole time, sneakin in and out of her dorm. Then she'd come see me fight in Tulsa and travel with me to Kansas and places. The first fight where she saw me do my stuff was at the Tulsa Fairgrounds.

"Baby, I didn't know you were so good. You're too popular for me," she told me after I came out of the dressin room with another win.

Jane remembers it different. "He had this uncanny gift for quickness," she likes to tell anyone but me. "His eye-hand coordination enabled him to slip punches that were amazing. His instinct was artistic . . . he could see what was coming before most fighters even knew what they were throwing.

"But James was born with a generational curse — he was born with too good of a heart and this hurt him in boxing. He'd back off if he knew his opponent was gettin hurt too much . . . he wouldn't ever be able to break someone's neck. Too much heart to go all the way to the top."

I started lovin her more than boxing and that's when the trouble started. Trainers and managers don't want no women around messin things up for their fighters . . . and I was in love with the wrong thing.

When I left for Chicago, I'd call her all the time. Spendin $120 a month for the phone bill was nothin. It was one of those once-in-a-lifetime love affairs. Before I knew her, my bowels never moved like most people's do in the mornin, but after I met her, every mornin my digestion system was runnin smooth. Like I said back then, I couldn't remember my name. She'd done somethin to me that drove me stone insane.

We got married in 1980 after I kayoed Domingo Deilia in the fourth and I was gettin ready to train for the Weaver fight; soon after that, she came to see me in Chicago since she'd decided to keep workin for an insurance company in Tulsa. I was takin her to the airport when she threw me a curveball.

"James, I think I'm pregnant."

"Baaaaaabbbbby, really?"

"Yeah, James, and if I am, this girl or this boy is going to be some special child. I can feel it."

She got that right. We named her Iciss after the Egyptian princess Isis I'd seen in the cartoon *Ole Mighty Isis* in the late '60s. But when Iciss Tillis was born in 1981, after Melanie and I divorced, I wouldn't be around. Jane Fonda stayed with the name Isis like we'd agreed on, but went with a different spellin. I still like to think of her as my Isis, my Egyptian princess of beauty. I helped Jane pay off an $8,000 hospital bill for complications durin the birth and then went back to Chicago. That's no way for a first-time father to act.

I didn't know how to act back then, gettin mad about lots of things, never knowin how to cool off, and she'd get jealous over little things. With all the trainin and pressure from my manager and trainer, we just couldn't make it last. I was stupid but I had me a career and that's all that was drivin me.

Jane and me only lasted for two or three months. Oprah Winfrey's attorney, Jeff D. Jacobs, got the papers together for a divorce.

But I was still in love with her and that cost me a lot of fights. It was like my mind was half in the ring and half in Tulsa with Jane. We was like Samson and Delilah.

Pretty women would be throwin themselves at me after the fights, before the fights. One good-lookin lady told me, "Baby I can make love with ya all night long."

"Baby, I'm not a teenager no more. It's gonna depend on how much Vitamin E I can get my hands on. I can't do this," I answered. I was still thinkin about my true love. I wasn't gonna kill myself for Jane Fonda like no Romeo and Juliet or nothin, but I was really in love.

But in 1982, one year after Iciss was born, I married another pretty woman named Gail Davis — hey, I wouldn't marry nobody that looked like the Phantom of the Opera or nothin. But we was only married for three or four months too. Them damn women just couldn't be quiet long enough for me to think. I had to think all the time, stay focused on the fight. I needed my women to just sit there and be quiet, not bother me, but I guess they didn't see it my way.

I kept tryin to see Jane when I'd get back to Tulsa and even though she was seein another guy, I called her anyway. In the meantime, I'd found me a good friend named Eva Beard — Eva the Beava I liked to call her — who was encouragin me, gettin me through the hard times with Melanie. When she had to move outta her house, I told her to move in with me, that we oughta get married. Less than a year later, she said "I think I might be pregnant, James."

"How you know?"

"A woman knows."

"Well, it's kinda bad timin but I betcha you'll make us a boy — you already made two for somebody else. But baby, here's some money if ya wanna go take care of it . . . you know."

I gave her the choice but, thank the good Lord, she got talked out of it by an elder in the church and by my mama. Yessir, Mama had a fit when she found out Eva might get herself an abortion.

"I told James, 'Baby, I'm gonna do this by myself,'" Eva says. "I told God, 'I'll leave this in your hands.' Ya know, it's when we get outta the way that God does somethin about it. James bubbled over when he found out it was a boy — looked jus like 'im too. Tillis took care of the hospital and doctor's fees but when I was in my ninth month with our son, Jamie, him and Melanie got back together. Can you believe that?

"Tillis always helped us out, though, when he could. Any time he'd get paid for a fight, he was over at my place, handin me $100 cash, $500 cash, one time $2,100 cash. He still wanted to be a part of that child's life, still wanted to look out for me and Jamie. Me and Melanie became real good friends, too, after a while. I'd do Iciss's hair, babysit her. Melanie and me never let go of our love for Christ. I knew everything would work out as long as I was on my knees. God can make a blessin out of a real mess, ya know."

While I was watchin Eva's belly get bigger and bigger with my first son, Jamie, I couldn't get my mind offa Jane Fonda.

"Baby, I'm still in love," I told her when I went over to see her. So we got married again. Thought this time it could work.

Four years, one ranch with horses, calves, tractors, and trailers later, we called it quits. We had all kinds of problems. I didn't trust her, I wasn't mature, I'd give Mama $1,000 for a car and pay off her house, spendin money like I'd never seen it before. When I'd get me a royalty check from *The Color Purple*, like about $1,000, I'd keep $300 and give the rest to Mama. I bought three cars for her — a '71 Plymouth, a '79 Nova, and a '75 Electra 225, helped her put money down on a blue Lincoln too. Guess I was like a little kid in a toy store for the first time, a cowboy store with cowboy hats and little horses and little trailers to put the horses in and big cars for Mama. Anybody need money? I'd give it to 'em. But it cost me my third marriage.

In '89, I was sparrin with Tyson, who was gettin ready to fight Carl "The Truth" Williams. We'd gone to Hilton Head,

South Carolina, to train. It was there that I'd see the prettiest damn green eyes I ever seen.

I'd gotten up early the mornin after we'd arrived since I hadn't seen my surroundins in the daylight, needed to check it out at 7 a.m. As I was headin out the front door of the hotel, I saw her.

"Good God Almighty, looka yonder. Fireman ain't gonna get it, somebody call the law." It was my *Color Purple* line and she was just the right one to tell it to.

"You can catch fish without a hook, you can make a blind man see, you can stop traffic at rush hour, Lord Almighty!" I kept it goin. She was smilin now, those cat eyes doin a job on me.

Her name was Evette Williams and I knew I wanted her to be all mine. In the meantime I had to go to Ohio to continue trainin with Tyson. Don King had a different thing in mind.

"You ain't workin hard enough, Tillis. It just ain't happenin."

"What you mean DK? I'm workin, man."

"Nope, I'm sendin you home."

I was mad, disappointed, embarrassed, and depressed all at the same time. I'd been tryin to come back but my head just wasn't in it — it was back in South Carolina with a green-eyed babe.

"No DK, I quit," I told that nigger the day I walked out on him. I'd walked out on one of my best friends, knowin I just couldn't get it together.

I flew down to South Carolina that night, grabbed me my woman, who I thought I loved, huggin that nice build and kissin those pretty lips right in the airport where she picked me up. After we got married, we headed back to Oklahoma where I just wanted to settle down with a nice wife. It wasn't long before I found out I'd be seein me a different woman — and I don't mean I was gonna be cheatin on nobody.

We hadn't been in town long when Evette and me visited

Mama's church down in the basement of Mama's house. All my family was there and I was prouder than a game rooster showin off my new wife. But I looked around at her and I couldn't believe it. She was shakin, tremblin all over her body, her eyes rollin back into her head and from side to side. What had gotten into my new woman? I thought maybe she was havin some kinda seizure or somethin.

I followed her stare and I realized she was gettin the hots over some guy in the room. We'd only been married for a few days and she'd found another man, a crazy look in her eye. It was my brother Barry. Later he told me that she tried to get him to go with her outside and lay down in the weeds, throwin herself on him, him pushin this crazy fool off him. I didn't know what I'd married.

A few nights later I was combin out her pretty black hair. I always like to do that with my women, them sittin in front of a mirror lookin at both of us, a husband combin out his new wife's hair. Romantic, huh? The comb hit some kind of bumpy thing under her hair, a scar on top of her head.

*What's this?* I was kinda afraid to ask. Maybe some other boyfriend had come after her with an ax, maybe she'd done it to herself.

I kept combin. Then I hit it again. "What IS this?" I asked her, really wantin to hear her story now.

"What? That ole scar up there? Why, that's just a bump I got when I fell on my head when I was little or somethin." She didn't say nothin more and I wasn't gonna ask.

*Yeah, you probly got dropped on your head by your daddy and that's why you so crazy.*

Maybe it was that scar or her bein a nymphomaniac or her stealin money from me that made me want to call off that marriage but whatever it was, we quit seein each other in 1989, right after she got pregnant, and two years later we finalized the divorce. I never seen our baby, my daughter Donna, who's now ten years old. It breaks my heart, but her mama was some crazy woman. On a scale of one to ten, I'd say she was a 12 when it comes to that body and those eyes but, man, when it comes to the head department, she's not even on the scale.

I was in some kinda sad shape by this time, tryin to get into the movies, doin some exhibitions but knowin that the boxing game was comin to an end. So on New Year's Eve I decided to drive my brown El Camino to my Aunt Joyce's. Thing was — she lived in Los Angeles and I was in Tulsa, Oklahoma, but I did it anyway. I made it to Amarillo before the alternator went out. Got that fixed, then it was the voltage regulator. It was gonna be a helluva new year. Next it was the modulator, and between Montoya and Albuquerque, New Mexico, it was the solenoid. By this time I only had $80 in my wallet but a Mexican kid who was helpin me out was good enough to take $20 and a picture of me and Ali I had in my suitcase.

After finally makin it to L.A., gettin me different promoters, doin an exhibition fight with Larry Holmes in Indonesia, doin comedy shows on the side, throwin the Tommy Morrison fight in Atlantic City, and gettin put in jail, I met me another woman. This one was straight in the head. I'll love her forever.

I parked right by her brown '86 Pontiac 6000 at the Flying Fox in L.A. and didn't even know it at the time, didn't know my next woman was waitin inside for me, and neither did she. The Temptations were singin "The Way You Do the Things You Do" over the speakers and I was dancin with some skinny girl when I saw a fine-lookin woman raisin her eyebrows at me. *Uh oh.*

"James 'Quick' Tillis is my name. I came over here to talk to you. Before I leave, I wanna know your name, address, and telephone number," I demanded. "Ain't you a fine young thing. What's your name, baby?"

"Lenita. . . . What's yours?"

Guess she had a short memory so I'd hafta tell her again.

"J.D. the Walker, the boss talker."

"You really somethin else."

"That's right, baby. I'm outta sight."

After our first dance, the rest is history. She gave me her card, told me she was some kinda lawyer or somethin.

When I called her on Monday, her only words were "uh huh, uh huh," like she didn't remember nothin. When I called her on Tuesday, it was the same, real mean and cold. When I called her on Wednesday, she sounded a little nicer. By Thursday, she was a real good friend, and by Friday, it was, "I'm having a party tonight. You wanna come?"

But when I got to 2111 Burnside in mid-city L.A., there was 20 guys standin outside her house sellin dope.

"Tell him to go, Mom," her son said when I walked up in my cowboy hat and Nocona boots. He was lookin at me like I was some crazy dude off the streets.

"No, nigger," she told him, "I wanna talk to this nigger."

"That's OK, Lenita, I don't want no trouble or nothin," I told her when we got inside, outta the way of them 20 guys.

"NO, I don't want you to go, I want you to be with me."

Her mother didn't take no quick likin to me either. When I went with her to Park Hills Church, she had to get somethin straight.

"So, where you livin?" her mama asked me with this suspectin look in her eye. She'd seen some men's size-54 suits in her daughter's closet.

"Uh, . . . uh, with Lenita, ma'am," I told her just when Lenita walked up to join us.

"Why, that's disGUSTing."

"Oh, but Mother, it's good, goddamn, it's good. Mother, I'm a grown woman by now. I can make my own decisions, don't you think?"

Lenita's mother called her own husband disgustin too. Said he was "old, disGUSTing, and ugly." I have to go along with her, he did look jus like the Grinch who stole Christmas.

Married Lenita in '92 and we had us some good times, got no complaints. She's good in what she does, a sports and bankruptcy attorney, even knows Diana Ross, went to high school with her. Later, Lenita became my manager, helpin me with all the legal stuff. But when I told her in '98 that I had to move back to Oklahoma or I'd go crazy — L.A., with all the smog and traffic, ain't got no seasons, no prairies — she just couldn't do it. Man, she can read all kinds of big thick books and learn everythin in 'em but she can't remember how to put a blanket and a saddle on a horse. I like to tease her bout that. We're still the best of friends but I filed for divorce in '99. I belong here in Oklahoma, woman or no woman.

# CHAPTER 11

# MY HERO

I know Steven Spielberg, Oprah Winfrey, Danny Glover. I stood in the same ring with Larry Holmes, Sugar Ray Robinson — Candy Man sweet to the bone. I sparred ten rounds with "The Greatest," Muhammad Ali, followin him to the gym in his Rolls Royce, runnin every red light he hit. And I'll never forget these people, these idols, my friends. But it's not one of them who's my hero. And after all the women I've had and known, I have only one woman I owe my life to. Mama. Rose Marie Tillis. Sister Tillis. Mama Tillis. Ya see, she wasn't just my hero. She was a hero to everyone whose life was touched by her.

Mama's mother, Olivia, died right in front of her, when Mama was just nine years old. That was when Mama saw her first vision — a woman was lookin at her in the mirror and then Olivia gagged, the breath sucked right out of her.

What happened after that I wouldn't ask on nobody. But like the Good Book says, "What was meant for evil, God meant for good." Mama was headin down a hell of a road but the hand of God would never leave her.

The family of five kids got ripped apart after Grandma Olivia passed. Some got sent off to Texas, some to Arizona. That tore Mama up so bad that she cried every day for her sisters and brothers; it was the only family she knew and she was dyin inside until she could pull 'em all back together, like a mother hen that can't find her chicks. She got put in her Aunt Hassie's house where she lived with Hassie's other children, but Hassie hated Mama for buttin in on her life. She made sure Mama would never forget it, forcin her to clean the floors, wash the dishes, and do the laundry for the family of nine. Some damn Cinderella story.

But that didn't keep Mama from doin her schoolwork late at night after all the piles of laundry been folded. She had the determination that she'd later give to me — she WOULD graduate and she WOULD hold her head up high. When she walked across that Booker T. Washington stage with a broken shoe floppin on her heel, an old, ugly dress under her robe — Mama never had a new dress — and not nobody out in the audience there for her, it didn't matter none. She was proud to be wearin that cap and gown. Nobody was gonna keep her down even if her heart was breakin inside.

Mama saw her ticket out of that Cinderella house by marryin Daddy, a nice-lookin guy who had a good job cuttin meat at the Mayo Hotel in Tulsa. But Mama didn't know she'd be travelin deeper into hell — 550 Virgin Street, the colored section of town. Five kids was born in that house, three bedrooms with two, three, or four children sleepin in one bed, anythin to keep us from sleepin down on the floor with the rats and roaches.

It was Daddy's drinkin that started it all.

I don't remember a lot of the stuff that went on with my older sisters, Glenda and Olivia. But Glenda don't forget nothin.

"When Mama was carrying Olivia," she says, "she had to sleep on the floor of the cold kitchen wrapped up in a sheet. You see, Daddy beat her so much when he got home from drinkin that she didn't want to be in no bed with him. And the reason that it was so cold in the house is because he'd knocked out the doors and windows in a rage. She told me later, 'Glenda, if this is a girl, I'm goin to name her Olivia after my mama.' And it was a girl. And she did name her Olivia. And ever since then, when Mama had some crisis, her mother, Olivia, would appear to her and later to the kids. It was like she was lookin out for her daughter and grandbabies.

"One night Grandma or an angel kept Mama alive. It was before I was born, and Daddy'd done gone crazy. All four girls remember it.

"I'll never forget, Mama had on her white slip that night," Olivia says. "Daddy had been drinking his whiskey and hit Mama on the head with an ashtray, making her bleed bad. I usually was scared of Daddy, him hitting Glenda with combination locks from her school locker, and wouldn't try to mess with him but when I saw that blood on her white slip and her staggering around from him hitting and kicking her, I tried to fight back.

"'SIT DOWN! SHUT UP!' I remember him yellin at me. And even though I was wanting so much to help Mama, to wipe off that blood that was running down her slip, I couldn't do nothin.

"'SIT THERE!' he yelled at us girls who was sobbing and shaking. He made us line up on our white couch in the living room, not a move or we'd get what Mama had got.

"'GET OUT!' He kicked her out of the house that night in her white slip, pregnant, bruised, and covered with blood. It was February and no one was around the cold dark streets at three in the morning except for an angel. Somehow that angel led her to a lady's house up the street who was there waitin for Mama. Probly saved Mama's life that night."

Even though Mama came from one hellhole and lived in

another one on Virgin Street, nobody'd ever know. She was a mighty proud woman, teachin all her kids to hold their heads up high. Mama's favorite words to us were, "You CAN . . . you CAN do it," and then she'd go starch the girls' clean white blouses, iron the 25-cent dresses she'd bought for them at the resale shop, press their ugly, thick hair, and shine our Oxfords for church — of course mine would just come back covered in dirt from kickin one of my cousins. None of us kids ever went without celebratin a birthday; we always had some kind of fresh-baked pound cake or chocolate birthday cake for us, made from scratch, Mama makin us all feel real special. Poor but special.

When Daddy moved out, Mama started cleanin houses for rich ladies, catchin the bus down south to fancy brick mansions on Memorial and 28th street, but it wasn't enough. Since we had to depend on "commodities" — I hated even the sound of the word — I was so embarrassed that I'd try to hide the fact from my friends, even though most my friends had 'em too. Spam, prunes, raisins, rolled wheat, cornmeal, big chunks of yellow cheese, flour, lima beans, chipped beef, powdered eggs. We'd tease each other that if you ate them powdered eggs instead of fresh ones, everyone would know it from the water runnin down your chin. Them eggs used to make me vomit if I didn't have no molasses to pour on 'em. Sometimes we'd have a special dinner with real chicken, and if there wasn't enough to go around, and there usually wasn't, Mama would give her piece to me. Always sacrificin for her kids.

My brother Barry says that now we would be called a "DYS-functional family." If it wasn't for God's hand and Mama's strong spirit, we would have starved to death or died of the cold. Daddy'd left us, and our refrigerator was usually empty except when the commodities came or other groceries appeared in the kitchen from friends.

I hated bein poor so much that sometimes I'd try to take care of business myself. I was only 10 or 11 but I'd figured out how I could bring home some money for Mama — stealin bicycles, or at least some of their parts. So one day I decided I'd seen enough of those commodities for a week and jus started runnin down the street. Trouble was, I went a little too far that day. I'd gone to the REALLY bad neighborhood, the wrong neighborhood inside the wrong neighborhood, if ya know what I mean.

"Help! Help!" I shouted to Mama, runnin faster than a calf with a burr up its ass, three of the meanest kids in the wrong neighborhood right behind me, shiny handlebars and a red Schwinn seat crunched under my arm.

But Mama didn't see no reason for comfortin me at the time. "You're NOT going to fight those kids," she told me with her meanest voice, hands on her hips, lookin straight into my eyes. "Aren't you ashamed of yourself goin and stealin like that, Junior?"

"But Mama, I . . . I . . . ," I cried, tears spittin outta my eyes, "I did it — "

"You stealin, Junior, that's what you doin, why you — "

"Mama, I wanted to get some money so we — " More tears and bawlin. "So maybe we c-c-could eat st-st-eak tonight."

I'll never forget the look in Mama's eyes when she seen my face and heard those words comin outta her son. "Oh, BAby, ya don't have to do no stealin for our family. God'll take care of His sheep . . . God'll take care of His flock. Thank you, Jesus." It was gonna be all right after all. Mama always felt bad after that day and if I remember it right, those evenin meal-times looked better after that.

And then there was the ghosts.

Mama'd always told us that 550 Virgin Street was haunted, but I didn't have no eyes to see the spirits. Mama, Angela, Sheryl, and Olivia did, though.

Mama called them familiar spirits, spirits that travel between time. For the longest time, my sister Angela couldn't sleep in the dark, had to have all the lights on in her bedroom.

"We was seein ghosts all the time on Virgin Street," Angela tells us kids as we sit in Sheryl's house talkin about Mama. "I remember the night that Glenda was pressing her hair, all excited and everything cuz she was gettin to go see the Jackson Five concert in Tulsa. She'd promised me I could go with her if I helped her get ready. Found out later she was lyin, but I was reachin through the curtain that was hanging up with thumb-tacks — that was our closet — and that's when I saw him. A blond-headed boy wearing little blue velvet shorts with three buttons on each side running up to the waist. He had on a short blue jacket with a collar trimmed in gold, white kneesocks, and black buckle shoes.

"'Hi, my name's Peter. I've been here a while,' he said. I turned to tell Glenda, and then he was gone. Weirdest thing, though. I saw *Unsolved Mysteries* just a few months ago and I was sitting there with a friend. They started talking about ghosts and mentioned this little boy from the 1700s that some people seen. A commercial came and I started describing that boy to my friend. It was the same boy.

"'How'd you know what he looked like?' my friend asked me, sittin there with her mouth wide open.

"'It was him,' I told her. 'The blonde boy in the blue velvet shorts and the black buckle shoes. I'll never forget him.' I guess those people on *Unsolved Mysteries* won't either."

One night Angela saw a woman scratchin on the window outside where I slept, hands bleedin, face white and scared.

Another time she heard a ziiiinnnngggggg sound in the back-yard by the clothes hangin and flappin. Ziiiiinnnggg. She heard it again and when she turned around an old Indian arrow was sittin there on the ground. Nobody there but the clothes flappin in the wind. And Sheryl saw Grandma Olivia in the livin room one night, dressed in an Oxford shirt and a long skirt, standin by the Cape Cod curtain and the water cooler that sat in the window, curlin her finger up and tellin her to come. No words, just movin a finger, *come.*

The cellar door would close by itself when there wasn't no wind around and Angela saw ghosts down there. Never did like that place much. My sisters tell me that my black iron bed used to shake when I was sleepin in it. I never noticed. Nothin could wake me up, not even a ghost.

"I'll never forget the rainy night that Mama let that angel into our house," Angela says. "It was storming real bad outside, and Mama and me was in the bathroom looking out the window.

"'Who's that lady in the uniform walking down the street, Mama . . . over there, by the hedges?' I asked her.

"'I don't know but she's gotta be awful cold and wet,' Mama told me. Pretty soon we heard a knock.

"Mama talked to that woman in the white uniform for a while. Never did know what they said to each other. When they were done talkin, I watched the woman walk back down the street and then she just disappeared in thin air. She was there and then there was nothin. Mama had entertained an angel, I'm sure of it."

When we finally left Virgin after eight years, we moved to a house on Frankfort with Mama's new husband, Jerry Thomas Fullbright. We was still in the colored section but we had lots of things there we'd never had before — full-course meals with roast and potatoes, a barbershop for Mama in the basement that later became "Sister Tillis's Church," a garden, and three more kids. Now we made 9.

My brother Barry looks back on that time. "Ya know, when Mama left Virgin, she got out of bondage. Mama locked that bondage and threw away the key. She sealed us as sisters and brothers for life — that seal can't be broken. She was out of sight when she did that . . . she was out of sight. Brought life to our family, that's what she did. We'd been dysfunctional before that, but when we moved out we began to have our identity. James 'Quick' Tillis hit the set, Mama's ministry took off. It was God's timing, that's what it was. God's timing. She got outta slavery."

Mama never called her other three kids "step-kids." They was just her kids and we was all her family. But then so was everyone else she ever met. I'm amazed when I think back and realize all the people she touched, all the lives she changed. I can't remember a Friday night growin up without some stranger sleepin in our house. She didn't turn away nobody. They'd be doped up on crack, starvin to death out on the streets, old women, drunks, pregnant teenagers with snotty, stinkin kids. Mama didn't care none.

"Mama, you don't know these folks. Aren't you afraid they'll kill you or somethin?" I asked her once when I'd come in after a high-school football game.

"Junior, I don't fear nothin. 'The Lord is my light and salvation; Whom shall I fear?' Let 'em sleep it off now," she'd say and then she'd go stir the pot of pinto beans that'd always be cookin on the stove for her friends.

But if people wanted food and shelter at Sister Tillis's, they knew they'd have to be up at 4:30 a.m. for prayer and Bible time. Even after some of her kids moved out, she'd call us on the phone — 4:30 sharp — time for prayer with the family. If she couldn't be at one of my fights, she'd call me right before I left my motel room. Time to pray with Mama.

"Every day of my life, Mama kept me in my right mind," Olivia tells us. "Mama would call me up hours before I had to be at work and say, 'Olivia, let's pray together. We need to pray for this broken man here on my floor this morning.

"'OK, Mama,' I'd say. You could never say no to Mama."

I tried lots of times to tell Mama about how tough it was but I just couldn't talk to her about it. She knew, though. Mama was my strength. Whatever I wanted to do, she was the one who pushed me to do it. "Sure, it can be done. You CAN do it," she'd tell me before the really tough ones, like the Tyson or Shavers fight. Then she'd get out her black big-print King James Bible with the gold letters on it and the big R on the side and read somethin from it while she rubbed my forehead gentle like with her anointed olive oil. "Protect James tonight, Lord Jesus. Give him YOUR strength, YOUR power tonight as he steps into that ring."

Mama came to see me fight eight fights in Chicago, but I didn't know how sick she really was until my sisters sent me an airplane ticket to come home in January of '95, just a few days before Martin Luther King Day.

"That ain't my mama," I remember tellin my sisters when I walked down the hall of Mama's house to the back bedroom where she was layin in bed, that 105-pound body that used to be 200 pounds hidin under the white sheet. I tried to keep from cryin but when I sat there feedin her some baby food that afternoon for lunch, lookin into her jaundiced eyes, I couldn't take it.

"Mama, Mama," I was cryin just like a baby, like the baby it looked like I was feedin. "Mama . . . Ma —"

"I ain't goin to git to eat if you keep crying like that, Junior."

I kinda laughed and wiped the snot off my face. My mama was dyin and I couldn't do nothin about it but keep feedin her baby food.

With me bein in Los Angeles tryin to get back into the fightin scene or the movie scene, hopin to hit a lick, I wasn't there to see Mama get even worse, but my sisters saw it. Angela says there had been somethin about the year 1994 — all the girls were already seein signs but nobody wanted to face it, especially Mama. First it was the yellow in her eyes, then it was the pounds she was losin — she gave away her black skirt to Sheryl when she couldn't wear it no more cuz it would just fall off. It was Mama wantin to sleep at Angela's house on the floor right in front of the air conditioner on a hot August night, wantin to see her breath, it was so cold. Then it was the phone call from the doctor.

"Mama came in that day after working her day job cleaning houses," Angela remembers. "It was a bad day, the mean old woman she worked for had been cussin her out, chewin her up and spittin her out like tobacco. But Mama'd never paid her much attention.

"I heard the phone ring . . . then I heard Mama crying, sobbing like nobody's business," Angela tells me. "'Yessir, I know,' she told the doctor. 'Yessir . . . yessir. I shoulda tole them. That bad . . . that bad.' She'd been told she had pancreatic cancer and it was spreading through her like wildfire. She hadn't had no money to go see the doctor earlier, hadn't been able to eat right. Always givin her strength to her children . . . no strength left for her no more.

"'Mama? You all right?' I asked her.

"'Hallelujah. Hallelujah. Bless the Lord, oh my soul, and forget not all HIS benefits.' Mama, sayin scripture, crumpled on the cold floor, speakin in the Spirit, raisin her arms before

God. 'YES, LORD! God says not now, Lord. Not now. God says it's OK . . . not weary . . . not weary. Thank you, Jesus, thank you, Jesus. I can do ALL THINGS through Him who strengthens me. HalleLUjah.'"

Soon after the bad news, Mama and the girls got a call from Sheryl. December 12, 1994. Sheryl's daughter had had a baby, Jesiah Quinn Jones, and the baby was turnin gray. The baby was dyin.

"Mama, you gotta help her. Please. Help her," Sheryl screamed out when she saw Mama come runnin down the hall in her red tennis shoes, her weight now down to almost 100 pounds. "He's dyin, Mama. He's dyin."

"When Mama was there with her children, Mama connected. She was our strength, she was the one we turned to when anything went wrong. Mama always knew what to do and who to go to," Sheryl says. "Fourteen years earlier, Glenda's daughter had had a stroke at the age of 14. Mama told Glenda, 'Let me take care of this. I'm goin to start praying.'

"Later when the doctors gave up on her and released the girl from the nursing home with no hope but severe brain damage — 'never be like other children,' they said — Mama took the girl in her arms and kept prayin. A few months later, the doctors couldn't believe what they saw. No sign of brain damage on the X-rays, nothin. Sheranda is now 32, healthy, with two children. It was always like that with Mama. Trusting and relying on God alone."

"I saw some woman that I'd never seen before walk down the hall of the hospital," Barry remembers of the day his nephew was dyin. "She walked right by us, we was crying and praying in the Spirit. That lady came up to us a few minutes later and said, 'I can help that baby if you'll let me.' We didn't know what to think, but about that time the nurses came over and shut the blinds where the baby was. We thought he was dead.

"Found out later that the baby had something, I forget the name of it, where his intestines were messed up, backing up into his lungs, acting like pneumonia. Somehow that lady got in there with the doctors and went with them to two different hospitals where they tried to keep him alive."

Sheryl interrupts, "Mama kept sayin, 'We're not gonna accept anything negative, ya hear?' and she'd keep praying in the Spirit, fightin the devil. That baby lived and is five years old today, doin just fine. We know now that Mama exchanged her life for that baby's, her life for her own great-grandchild."

We all knew God could heal Mama if He wanted but He wanted her home with Him, sittin by the throne of Jesus. "In My Father's house are many mansions; if it were not so, I would have told you. I go to prepare a place for you," she would tell her congregation every Sunday mornin for as long as she could speak the words. But Mama still wasn't ready to go. She had so much to do for her kids and for them that was in need of her.

"Mama refused to give in to her sickness," my sister Penny tells us. "She'd crawl out of bed on Sunday mornings so weak she could hardly stand, slip her robe over her nightgown, and walk down those cold stairs into the basement of her house where she had her church.

"'Mama,' I'd try to tell her, 'you're too weak. You can't keep doin this.'

"'I can do all things . . . through Him . . . who . . . strengthens . . . me,' she'd say, gasping for breath, her lips chapped from the morphine, her eyes showing the pain. 'I will stand on . . . the . . . battlefield . . . until the . . . battle . . . is done.' But after a few months, she couldn't get no strength to climb out of bed and go down those stairs. So when people came by the house, she'd pull out her King James Bible with the words of Christ in red and the gold R on the side and read to them from her hospice bed. Nothin could keep Mama from sharin Jesus with a lost world. Then she slipped into a coma. She was in and out of that coma from then on."

It was January 17, 1995, when God gave Penny a vision. "I saw Mama with thousands of other people, everyone else dressed casual but Mama. There she was standing out in this huge field like a band that plays for the football games. All the saints were surrounding her with Mama right in the middle of 'em. Standin there in a long-sleeved white robe.

"'Mama! There's Mama!' I shouted when I saw her in that field. I was pointin my finger at her, 'Mama! Mama! There you are!' I was just so happy to see Mama in the middle of all them people. Then she turned around and, just like the vision of Jacob, she started walkin up to heaven. But not on a ladder . . . it was a big plane with stairs coming down. On each stair there was angels kneeling down. Mama just kept climbing them stairs, going past those angels. Then the stairs and Mama disappeared. She was with Jesus and I felt sooooo good."

Others in our family had visions. Sheryl saw Mama in the Spirit with Mama carryin some brown high-top shoes all tied together with their shoestrings. "Come on baby," Mama told her. "Put on your travelin shoes. We're gonna march for JEsus!" And she walked off down an aisle, singin and shoutin to the Lord.

In February '95, a month after Mama died, I had a dream where everythin was white. Mama and me was sittin on a snow-white love seat in a snow-white room with snow-white clouds all around us, just me, Mama, and for some reason, Johnny Mathis.

"Mama . . . Mama? You in paradise?" I remember askin her.

"Yes, son, I'm in paradise — "

"Oh, thank you JEsus!" I cried out from my bed and then I woke up. I've never felt so good. Mama was in paradise with her Lord and Savior. I could finally rest knowin that.

Mama even had a vision that she tried to tell Angela about soon before she went into her coma.

"'Mama, look outside,'" Angela remembers tellin her while they was lookin out the front window of Angela's house. "'I think it's gonna snow tonight.' When Mama was so sick she used to love to look out the window . . . she loved windows and bright light. She was sittin in her favorite wingback chair in my living room under her favorite velour blanket.

"'Angela . . . listen . . . to me,' she tried to say, her breaths so shallow now.

"'Please, God, let your Spirit breathe for her. Breathe for her,'" Angela prayed.

"'Mama, don't you think it's gonna snow tonight? Don't you — '

"'Shut up . . . listen . . . listen. A man's coming . . . a doctor . . . to take the bed away . . . a nurse with . . . a clipboard . . . talkin to the doctor . . . angels gettin ready for me . . . big pretty wings . . . coming down the hall. Take me home.'"

It snowed later that night.

Mama was stayin at Angela's house. One day Olivia went to check on her, lookin in at her sleepin in the hospice bed. Olivia quickly turned around.

"Angela! Come quick. Barry! Come look!" she whispered down the hall at her sister and brother. "Come see!"

When they ran into the room, there was Mama layin in that bed, the sunlight shinin on her face. But it wasn't just any kind of sunlight. It was the shape of a cross on her forehead. Right there across her beautiful black face, a cross of God's light stamped on His saint.

"Man . . . that's beautiful!" whispered Angela.

"I believe," Barry said as he looked at Mama with that sign from heaven shinin for the three of them to see.

Mama held on to two things before she left us.

"My babies," she cried, right before she passed. "Danny . . . Shannon." She called for her grandson and her son, both locked up in jail. "Please . . . tell them . . ." Angela got on the phone and, by some miracle, the jailers had both Danny and Shannon on the other end of the phone with Mama within five minutes.

"Mama, it's me, Shannon. Mama . . . I love you SO much. Mama . . . it's time to go now. It's time to go," he bawled over the phone as he was dyin inside and Mama was dyin outside.

"Shan — " And then we heard her lungs collapse as she arched her back, her tongue stickin out tryin to find air, then there was the smell of blood and bowels loosenin. The whole family was right there by her bedside, Shannon and Danny on the phone. I guess you could say Mama knew how to leave this world in style, her whole family by her side — even the preacher was there, cryin by her bed, standin next to the doctor . . . and the nurse with the clipboard.

It was the second largest black funeral in Tulsa, close to a thousand people swellin out of the Faith Christian Fellowship. People I ain't never seen. Lines of black people, white people, Mexicans; prisoners who got out of jail and homeless people whose lives Mama touched were pourin out the door, chairs outside, people wall to wall. I'd never seen so many people at a funeral. And I've never seen so much food or so many flowers. Olivia said that there was enough cash left over from the funeral money to pay for three month's rent for Barry, who was livin in Mama's house. People I'd never heard of came by to give money. The funeral and the furniture Mama'd rented were all paid for in full. Mama Rose was their hero and mine. Penny later wrote some beautiful words about her hero.

*Mama.*
*Person of understanding, love, strength, kindness, encouraging.*
*Love for God and people, helped the less fortunate and fortunate.*
*Always made you feel welcome.*
*Vitality, wisdom, self-denial.*
*Didn't believe in wasting time.*
*Mother of many nationalities.*
*Soft-spoken but firm;*
*What she said, she meant, and it was so.*
*Warm arms of caressing.*
*If I had to choose a hero, it would be my mother.*
*Mama.*
*Bore all things, believed all things, hoped all things, endured all things, never failed.*
*Mama was love.*
*Love was Mama.*
*Mama, I love you so.*

*There's no need to cry and moan no more, sisters and brothers. Mama's where she wants to be. You was a strong soldier, Mama. You are my hero and now you're with yours.*

# CHAPTER 12

# SEEIN THE WORLD

I'm just a country boy who likes to wear my Stetson, my calf-ropin belt buckle, and my Nocona cowboy boots, and ride a horse out on a few acres. I love the outdoors, lookin at the stars on a clear night, watchin the trees change colors in the seasons. I lived in Los Angeles for seven years but I couldn't take it. They ain't got no seasons out there and there's too many people and smog. Give me a fall day in Oklahoma any time instead of all them palm trees, all them cosmoPOLitan people. Hell, nobody there goes to the bathroom outside, they so cosmopolitan.

But when I got into boxing, I got more than just trainin and fights. I'm country but I ain't from no cotton field. I've been around. I got to travel all over the world and I guess you could say that made me like my home even more.

My first big trip was back in '77 when I got to travel with the U.S.A. boxing team to Europe. I was ready to see the world, me and the other fighters on the team, like Thomas "Hit Man" Hearns. I had two fights over there, one in Germany and another in Sweden. I won both of 'em. We got to go to Norway, Finland, Sweden, and Germany, places a lot of my friends couldn't even find on a map. Hell, I couldn't find 'em on a map. I'd heard of them but I had no idea what to expect.

I was only 19 when I went so I don't remember all that much, but I do remember the people. I remember that if they don't like a fight, they clap, if they do like it, they whistle. They also don't know nothin bout breakfast. No biscuits, gravy, eggs, no hash browns. No, their idea of breakfast is just a hard roll or two and some dang butter. In my opinion, that ain't no kinda breakfast.

In 1985, I got the chance to fight Gerrie Coetzee in Johannesburg, South Africa. I wondered what it would be like to go to a country where some of my ancestors probably lived. I was real curious. When Willy B and me got off the plane, I looked around at the airport. I'd never seen so many black folks in one place. "Hey," I whispered to B, "I'm here with the REAL niggers now." We just laughed.

But what I first noticed when we got in the city and were walkin around was the black women. Gorgeous. I mean every one of 'em. Beautiful. I'd say 99.9% of 'em was flawless. They didn't take no baths but they all looked like a bunch of Lena Hornes walkin around. All day long I couldn't believe it.

"Man, she's pretty," I'd tell B.

"Man, she's prettier than HER," I'd say again, two seconds later, pointin to another Lena Horne.

"Man, she's even prettier!" Never seen nothin like it. I was thinkin I might just want to stay a few weeks longer after the fight was over. That is, until the next day.

Willy B and me had just gotten done eatin. The best thing for a fighter to do after eatin a big meal is to get that food digested, so we was out walkin the streets of Johannesburg, enjoyin the evenin. I noticed when we passed by an alley that there was two big dudes hangin out there, and I mean big — seven-foot-tall jet-black Zulus with some nice pearly teeth. When I looked at them again, one of 'em stared me right in the eye, licked his lips, and rubbed his stomach.

Man! I was out in the middle of the street. Them cannibals had me goin. Nobody's seen me walk as fast as I did that night. *Nigger, you'll never eat me, baby!* When I looked over my shoulder, they was peekin out from behind that alley wall, still smilin at me with them pearly white teeth.

"I know some of this black, greasy ass you'd LOVE to taste, but from here to Landross Hotel — it's gonna be one HELL of a race." And I hit the pavement never lookin back.

In 1987 I had me another scare, but this time it wasn't no cannibals — it was werewolves. I was fightin Frank Bruno in London and I thought it was just gonna be a normal mornin for me. At 5 a.m. I stepped out of the Holiday Inn Marble Arch for my usual mornin run in Hyde Park, gettin trained for the fight. It looked like one of them Count Dracula movies. Fog was movin all around them park benches and those brave people out there walkin around in their black coats. Count Dracula. Werewolves. Frankenstein.

*Shit, I'm not goin out there. I'll do my runnin later.* I went back to my room and crawled up under those covers. I wasn't messin with no werewolves at that time of mornin.

Four weeks later I was gettin my checkup for the fight. They'd told me to go to this certain buildin where I'd find the doctor. Problem was, the doctor's office was ten flights down in the basement. It was all dark when I got down there, a bunch of other fighters in line for their checkups. When someone knocked on the doctor's door, I heard this low, scary voice, the voice of Dracula himself, say, "Yeeeeeessssss?"

"Man, you guys," I told everyone in line. "I gotta be checked first. I'm sorry but you guys might leave me down here." They all fell out laughin but I didn't care. My big white eyes was shinin bright down in Dracula's dungeon and I wanted outta there fast.

Had me some fun after my checkup though. I found me a place in the sunlight to go get me some breakfast — didn't ever think the sun would look so good. When I got inside, there was Charlie Pride himself sittin in a booth havin him some eggs and toast.

"Hey, Charlie, are you a hillbilly nigger for real?" I asked him right when he was puttin his coffee cup to his mouth.

Haw haw haw. He almost threw up his coffee over that one. I like Charlie. He don't care what you call him. He knows how to have some fun with brothers.

I got to see Westminster Abbey and some ancient graves — with dates sayin 1156–1215, ya know, priests and kings buried there, so old you couldn't even read the names. Big Ben, Parliament House, Tower of London, Baker Street, places where Jack the Ripper walked, and if they hadn't sold London Bridge, I'da gotten to see it too. London was great.

I had me some fun times "down under" and in the outback, too, when I fought Joe Bugner in Sydney, Australia. I'd met a man named Jess Dunley flyin from Honolulu to Sydney and we'd been crackin jokes all the way there — and it's a long way. So when I saw this copilot come out of his cabin I couldn't help it. He had on this little airplane hat on his little head with little eyes and lips on his face.

"Hey, man, you look like a MOVIE star," I told him when he walked by me and my friend.

"Oh yeah? I do?" He thought this was his lucky day. "Who do I look like?"

"Why, you look just like Barney Rubble on *The Flintstones*." Jess and me thought we'd never stop laughin. Barney didn't think it was that funny.

Before the fight, I met this real pretty blonde lady in a restaurant across the street from where all the hookers hanged out. I decided to take her to see *The Color Purple* that was showin at the time. Of course I wanted to point out yours truly up on the screen with Oprah.

But when we went to a party after the fight that night, I had to warn Willy B off. He'd spotted the blonde too and was tryin to move in on her.

"B, go get your own action," I told him when I was gettin me a 7-Up. "I got me my girl. You go find your own."

But he kept tryin to get me to sit down between two other pretty girls while he moved in on the blonde. No luck, B. Her and me walked arm in arm outta that party and down the hall into my hotel room. I went in to take my shower, feelin like my luck was changin after a ten-round loss to Bugner.

She was sittin on the couch lookin real fine when I got out.

"Ya wanna kiss me don't ya, baby?" I asked her when I saw her just sittin there, kinda nervous.

"No, I don't. I'm not that kinda lady," she told me. THAT was a first and it would be the last. After all that fightin with B over her, I was not goin to see any action that night. I packed my bags that night feelin real sorry for myself in the outback, and headed home to my ranch in Tulsa where I knew the women loved me.

There was Indonesia, Brazil, and Vancouver. Indonesia had Ali and Kool and the Gang at the fight, an exhibition match with Larry Holmes. When I was trainin before the fight, I had a good time with Larry, who kept tryin to sing the song "My Girl" but instead of singin the words "My girl, I got sunshine," he kept messin around singin "My girl — me got sunshine." They tried to get me to sing but I just kept tellin them, "I cain't sing, I cain't sing. Larry, tell 'em. I cain't sing." I ended up recitin some Rudy Ray Moore stories. They loved it.

Edmonton in Canada's got the mall. Makes our malls in

Tulsa look like some ghetto malls. I even did some stand-up comedy shows in Edmonton, borrowin from my friend comedian Rudy Ray Moore.

"Hey, I got on the bus back home on my way to the gym. This man got on the bus after me — he had 'im a monkey. I said, 'Bus driver, do you allow monkeys on this bus?'

"'Nigger, if you go over there and sit down, no one will know you on here.'" Haw, haw, haw.

"Hey, I went to a white barbershop one time. 'Give me the Afro look, sir,' I told the barber. I fell asleep in the chair and when I woke up about an hour later, the cat had stuck a bone in my nose." Haw, haw. We had us some good times.

Sometimes I'd be gone for three months at a time. I loved seein the world but all that flyin made me tired. No, I ain't from no cotton field. I've been around, seein Dracula, Zulus, Lena Hornes, and Scandinavians in their wool hats, but I'm glad to be livin where I live and glad to be knowin who I know. Even if I am just an ole country boy from a place called Tulsa.

# CHAPTER 13

# HOMETOWN GLORY, HOMETOWN SHAME

Jesus said it himself, "A prophet is not without honor except in his hometown, and in his own household. . . . Truly I say to you, no prophet is welcome in his hometown." Now I know I ain't no prophet, but I know what it's like to make it big — bein loved by your hometown when you're on top then bein dragged in the dirt when you're on the bottom.

When I was makin it big in the amateurs, I had to work my butt off. When I turned pro, I had to work even harder. I had 50 cents in my pocket, one guy, Robert Hudson, who believed in me but didn't have no money, and a girlfriend and Mama back home who said I could do anythin I put my mind to. No help, no money from nobody.

Evander Holyfield knows what I'm talkin about. When he was tryin to find a sponsor for the Olympics and everyone was tellin him that he was too small to be a boxer, that he was "too nice to make it," he asked his wife, Paulette, "Why, baby, why? Why won't they believe in me? What else do I have to do?" Holyfield had become used to people doubtin him. But, just like me, "every obstacle was just another challenge that needed to be overcome."

"Forget them fools," I say. "They're just jealous." And I wish fighters could just forget about those people who don't believe in them, but the thing is professional boxers gotta have money to make it big. And to have money, ya gotta have people who believe in you. It was Jim Kaulentis that found me with a quarter in my pocket and he handed me two crisp one-hundred dollar bills. He believed in me and had money. Fighters gotta find both.

When I had four fights in Tulsa, they loved me. I drew people to the Tulsa Civic Center like ants runnin to a pile of sugar. Sell-out crowds, standin room only. Everybody had been hearin about me makin it big in Chicago. Like my friend Ronnie Warrior says, Chicago tried to claim me, but I was born and raised in Tulsa and I loved Tulsa, no matter how I was treated. I don't think nobody in Tulsa believed in me and my abilities except for Mama and my trainer Ed Duncan. But when I was on top, everyone in Tulsa made sure the world knew I was from a place called Tulsa, Oklahoma. It's a crazy world, just like Jesus says.

"Everybody loves a winner but not too many people can accept you when you lose," Kenny Lucas, who took me in before the Morrison fight, reminds me. "If you have something that comes out of your community, like you, then you should support it. A lot of people don't wanna say where they're from if that community hasn't supported them, but ya know, it's easy for people to judge outside the ring and they're real quick to judge because of a lost status — but they have no idea what it took to get to that point.

"It's not how you lose; it's how you fought the game. Hey, some of the greatest lose, but your community didn't accept you back then because you weren't a fighter from A to Z — you stopped off at J and even S. Heavyweights today come a dime a dozen, James. I commend you for just getting in the ring with those heavy, HEAvy people of that era."

Kenny looked out for me, and he wasn't even in Tulsa at the time, cuz he says he always believes in lookin out for a "homeboy." But I heard that even Chicago, my second home, treated me like a prophet when I was there. A guy I never even knew, Phil Flynn, who still works at the Mercantile Exchange and knows Kaulentis, talks about what a celebrity I was just workin the floor as a runner.

"All the money backers saw Quick Tillis as the future heavyweight champion of the world and were putting money in his pocket. He was the talk of the trading floor.

"But after the first big fight where he didn't do so well, Quick Tillis went from a buzzword to a letdown. He went from a hero to a goat."

Boxing's like that. You're all alone, and those people who treat you like God one minute, treat you like shit the next minute — people quickly forgot the 21 straight wins I had in Chicago and the 15 rounds I went with Weaver only to end up in a split decision. If you don't keep winnin, they turn against you. It's all about bein on top, makin the money.

I walked into Reuben Gant's office the other day. This is a guy who got a full ride to Oklahoma State University and played tight end for seven years with O.J. and the Buffalo Bills. Now he sits behind a desk at the Greenwood Chamber of Commerce; there's a sign out in the lobby that says "A vision without hard work is nothing but a daydream."

Yeah, Reuben's tryin to help Greenwood get back like it used to be in 1921 when Greenwood was called the Black Wall Street — the same area where 40 years later Daddy'd drink his corn whiskey while I sat on a barstool in the back of a bootleggin joint.

Reuben understands what I'm talkin about.

"I wouldn't be where I am today without sports," he tells me, lookin all spruced up in his clean shirt and pants, business cards sittin on his desk. "I had seven brothers and sisters but we were proud folks. We were never on welfare and Mom and Dad stayed together till they died.

"But segregation was at its peak when I graduated from Booker T. Washington High School, the school that never lost a football game in Oklahoma while I was there. When I got drafted to the Buffalo Bills, the community had something to grab onto. I was a proud symbol of the black community, of all the community. But football is a team sport that's very visible. Boxing isn't."

I liked this guy the more I sat there. He was my brother.

Reuben's been in big-time sports but he knows it's different when you're in it all alone instead of lettin the team take the fall.

"When you're in an individual sport like boxing, you're under a microscope. It's all about mano on mano, one on one. It's like that with college wrestling today. You don't see much of that. The only reason boxing has notoriety is because boxing is money."

Reuben admits that he don't know nothin about gettin hit in the face for money. But then again, a lot of boxers probably can't see gettin tackled for money either. "To each his own," he says.

He surprised me, though, when he told me one thing. "I've been to every state in the U.S. with the exception of Alaska and everywhere I went when I was playing ball, people would ask me where I was from.

"'Tulsa, Oklahoma,' I'd tell them.

"'Tulsa? Quick Tillis is from Tulsa.' I'd say six out of ten times people would tell me that. They usually remembered that Tillis was the first to go ten rounds with Tyson on ABC."

People are funny. Hometown glory, hometown shame, I call it.

"It's all about money," I said.

"Yes, money is important," Reuben said, "but it's also about influence. People want to rub shoulders with notoriety, popularity. It's not any different in Tulsa. People that I've never seen come up to me even today and talk to me like I was their buddy or something.

"Ya know, Tillis, people assume that just because we were professional athletes, that we must have made a million dollars. Do you know what the minimum salary for an NFL player was back in 1974? $12,000. People just don't know what they're talkin about. And the hardest thing to do is change people's perceptions, so why even try? Perception is reality to them.

"I'm comfortable with who I am — I really don't care if they think I have a lot of money or don't have a lot of money. What business is it of theirs anyway? The question is does Reuben Gant like Reuben Gant? Does Quick Tillis like Quick Tillis? You've done something a lot of us wish we'd done. If people don't give you respect it's out of envy. They didn't have the heart to do what you did. They're just thinkin, 'He did something I could never do.'"

Gant understands the difference, though, between playin football and boxing. It's called "a saving grace," and boxers ain't got none of it.

"Tillis, you probably remember that the Buffalo Bills were the worst team in the NFL during a two-year period when I played for them. But do you think people hated me or put me down for it? No way — it wasn't me that was losin, it was the team. Saving grace. It's different with boxing. When you're out in the ring like you were, all by yourself, there's no saving grace."

Back when Gant was tacklin and later when I was throwin punches, nobody knew nothin about Tulsa. If they did, it wasn't about no athletes or no professional teams. That's why I had to get out of Tulsa.

"Black athletes put Tulsa, Oklahoma, on the map," Gant tells me, lookin prouder than a game rooster. "In college during the '70s, I'd go West and the first thing they'd say about Tulsa was, 'Well, I didn't even know blacks lived in Tulsa.' The second thing they'd say was, 'How many oil wells do you have in your backyard?'

"I'd go East and they'd ask me if we still rode horses to school. But Reuben Gant, Quick Tillis, Wayman Tisdale, and John Starks put Tulsa on the map. These professional athletes meant visibility for our city. I could have lived anywhere I wanted to but I came back to Tulsa because of the support and encouragement I got growing up playing sports. I have to give back what they gave to me."

And I guess you could say that's why I'm back in Tulsa, too. I tried livin in Chicago and L.A. but it's just not the same. All I want to do is get me some land on a ranch outside of Tulsa, get me a few horses, and retire. I've paid my dues in boxing. It's time to enjoy the cowboy thing, the first love of my life.

But Lawrence Lakey, my personal Bundini Brown, my right-hand man who I met in Tulsa and took with me to Chicago, got some even meaner words when it comes to hometown glory and hometown shame. He thinks it has to do with "the crab syndrome, the black psyche."

"Tillis, it's the prophet not being honored in his own town. You were the closest thing to Ali I'd ever seen — the foot speed, the way you hit, your size and height — but the more you went up, the more the crabs, the black people especially, would pull you down. It's the black psyche, a sense of envy and disappointment about themselves. It's the negative legacy and history of the black community.

"You had more athleticism and skill than any Wayman Tisdale or John Starks. You were a local kid who was fightin for the WORLD heavyweight championship. You should have gotten great respect, but you'd get $50,000 to Holyfield's half million. I never felt like Tulsa gave you the credit you deserved. Man, so much is taken from a gladiator."

He was gettin on a roll now. Kinda makin me embarrassed but I was listenin.

"The public needs to know that this industry of boxing is dealing not only with money and fame but with people's LIVES. Kids need insight into all sports but especially boxing if they're thinkin about bein a fighter. More light needs to be shed on the game, and this message should be told to protect our future fighters. It's a tough world out there and not everybody can come through it like you did."

My friend Dr. Eric Mikel, who lives and works in north Tulsa and has him college degrees both in architecture and medicine, knows what Lakey means when he talks about that "negative legacy" stuff with our own people. He's been doctorin and supportin the north side for 15 years now, tryin to help the poor, but he's a livin example of the black community lookin down on their own. He talks about the racism thing, too.

"My community thinks I'm crazy tryin to be an entrepreneur. If I don't make it, they'll be the first to tell me, 'Yeah, you shouldn'ta been doin that in the first place.' They want me, the guy with four degrees, to be out pushin a broom, clockin in, sayin 'yessir' and 'no sir' to somebody. My daddy did that for years down at the Greyhound bus station, making a living for his family of four off tips, and he was adamant that his kids wouldn't be doin the same thing.

"But when I go to the bank and try to get a $5,000 loan for my office, they say no. When my white friend who just got out of dentist school goes and asks the bank for a $500,000 loan to get set up, they say, 'Sure, when do you need it?' When I designed the first two buildings of Tulsa Junior College on Apache which still stand there today, my boss made sure that he got them right over to the white man's architecture company, but didn't bother to get my name on those plans. I'm a living example — a lot of the white community won't let you get any further than they want you to get.

"And Quick, the same thing happened to you. As long as you were on top, they loved you. But when you fell, instead of choosing to clock in somewhere, you chose the streets with your dreams. Your heart is here with your own, you love to talk to the old woman on the street who's tryin to get by or the man who sells fruit at the intersection of Apache and Pine. You're like me, you're different and you have a higher goal, but they'll still say, 'Quick Tillis? He's jus a nigga that used to box.'"

Eva Beard, the mother of my son Jamie, saw it too. "It was crazy. When the white intern in the hospital found out who I gave birth to, he went hollering through the hospital halls, 'Tillis? That's the boxer's baby? The boxer's little boy! It's Tillis' first little boy!' When Jamie got a little older, I'd take him to the flea market and have to yell his name, 'Jamie Tillis, you get over here.' 'Tillis? Did you say Tillis?' people all around me wanted to know. We was some kind of celebrities just with the name Tillis.

"But it's our own community, the north side, that don't pay him no attention. Tillis and me went to a north side club one night, Brown Sugar it was called. They actually tried to beat him up with pool sticks. We went on down to south Tulsa to another club. Honey, they wanted to buy our meal THERE. The blacks ain't gonna give him no mind, he's not about nothin now cuz he's from here. If ya's from here, you'll never be no star. That's what's wrong with our race today. Them mens tearin down each other — they don't go tearin down the women, mind ya, they jus wanna go tearin down them other black mens.

"But what got me about Tillis," she says as she looks over at me with this big ole grin and still a sparkle in her slanted eyes, "is that no matter what he goes through he's got a peace of mind. Though the times are hard, he don't let nothin bother him. That's his real gift. If them guys was beatin up on me with some ole pool stick, I'd be lookin for a rock to throw at 'em. But you know what Tillis'd be doin when we was walkin off? Whistlin. He'd be whistlin some crazy Motown tune or a spiritual. I beat him with a purple heel one time, blood comin outta his arm and everything. Here's this big ole boxer could of beat me up good, but he'd just be standin there, his arms coverin his face, lettin me have at him. That's the thing about Tillis — he's slow to anger. Ain't too many mens let ya hit 'em like that. Sometimes his biggest problem is that he cares too much. That's been his downfall."

Another professional athlete you might know, a white guy who broke records as a pass receiver for the Seattle Seahawks and is a Pro Football Hall of Famer, came from Oklahoma City and now works in Washington D.C. as a real United States Representative. Steve Largent. Maybe you heard of him. But he ain't quite seein it like Dr. Mikel and Eva. He thinks that lots of people, not just the black community, wanna attack everybody who's successful.

"It's jealousy, I believe," Largent tells me. "But, personally, being told I could NOT succeed fanned my competitive flames. That's what drove me on. It's true that our culture today worships athletics and athletes. That just seems to be the way it is. And because of this, they can have quite an influence in the community."

I ain't mad at nobody. Like Jane Fonda says, I don't hold no grudges against nobody. I paid my dues and now I just wanna enjoy my cowboy livin.

"But, James," a former boxer and still a good friend, Ronnie Warrior, tells me, "there's no reason in the world why you shouldn't have been honored and been given support. There should be some kinda memento for the name of James 'Quick' Tillis and his career. You done a lot for Oklahoma fighters — you opened a lot of doors for the pros."

"Yeah, yeah, that's OK," I say.

"No, it ain't. I don't care what the press said then or says now — they never threw no punches, all they do is watch and write. Quick Tillis came out of Oklahoma even though Chicago tried to claim you. You put Oklahoma AND Chicago on the map for heavyweight champions of the world. You was kickin ass with Jim Kaulentis in the Windy City.

"There's no doubt," he continues. "Every heavyweight had to take the doorway to James 'Quick' Tillis in order to be considered legitimate for the world title. If they couldn't get past you, they wouldn't work out."

Some sportswriters did me good, writin words that've turned yellow in my scrapbook. It's just that your hometown forgets fast. "Quick Tillis is the kind of yardstick that experts use to gauge greatness in others," said one Sydney writer, Grantlee Kieza. "He handed the monstrous Mike Tyson the toughest fight of his life . . . and he constantly frustrated the 'bionic' right hand of Afrikaaner Coetzee in Johannesburg. . . . Survivors from Tyson's search-and-destroy missions are so rare that those who escape without broken bones are lauded, he says."

*No broken bones.*

*Not even a scratch, baby.*

"Those who are still standing at the final bell go into the record books."

*Still standin, still dancin — but not high in the record books.*

"'Those who demand a rematch see their psychiatrist,' he keeps saying about me."

*Tyson wanted the rematch and he got one later, but not the way I wanted, just an exhibition fight. And baby, I ain't never been to no psychiatrist.*

My friend Wayman Tisdale knows what it's like to be a nobody one day and a hero the next. He ain't actually from Tulsa but he moved here when he was four, him and his close family of six. Wayman's like me — his first love wasn't no sport, it was somethin else. Music. And when he was a six-foot-three-inch seventh grader who couldn't do nothin with no coordination, nobody wanted him around.

"When I shot an airball for Carver Junior High during the last few minutes of an important game, all the girls in the school hated me," Wayman says. "It was the darkest time for me as an athlete. I knew I didn't want anything like that to happen to me again. So it was either give up basketball or work harder. I chose to go at it hard. I went from sittin on the bench to being the number-one basketball player in high school, went to the Olympics in '84, got drafted by the Indiana Pacers in '85, and later was the first player in NCAA history to earn All-America First Team honors in my first three years with the Phoenix Suns. I went from being a sorry, clumsy guy to a hero all of a sudden." He laughs as he stands in his recordin studio, where he's fulfillin his first dream after all, me lookin up to HIM, even in my cowboy hat. Wayman's all right.

"But it's tough being an athlete and being a hero. I had the deadliest position, small forward, and had to go up against guys like Dr. J, Michael Jordan, James Worthy, Larry Bird, Magic Johnson. But because you're paid so much as a professional basketball player, everyone expects results. So you get criticized unfairly, and if you don't give back to the community the way people think you should, then they give you a hard time.

"You have to live with a bad rap — that's part of being a star. If you give, it's not what they wanted you to give. You see, I like to do things to help people, not just for the publicity. But if I try to please both sides, I can never win. That's why I always go back to my old neighborhood — go to my same church I used to go to, the same barbershop. I'm just regular me."

Wayman knows what I'm talkin about with Tulsa. Even if we didn't always get the glory, even if the shame came right behind sometimes, we both still like to be in our own town. And Tulsa's home to Tisdale too.

"Nobody has to honor me with some big parade like they do for athletes in the big cities. Everything's fake in the big city. Nothing's real like it is here. When I was in high school, Quick Tillis came to Booker T. Washington to see us kids. Man, everyone came running to get his autograph and stuff. But what amazed me about Tillis was that he was so cool, so down to earth. He'd been on TV boxing Mike Tyson but he just blended in with us kids, shadowboxing and stuff with all of us. People used to compare him to Ali back then and there he was, shadowboxing and just being who he was in his own hometown. That made a big impression on me.

"When kids want to know how they can make it big, even if they go to a rough school or live in a rough neighborhood, I tell them that I wasn't any different. I just didn't adapt to my environment. I didn't become a chameleon. Kids shouldn't let anyone else determine who they are gonna be. At the end of the day, it's all up to them. They'll have to look at themselves in the mirror and know that who they become is their responsibility, not someone else's.

"That's what made Michael Jordan superior, not just in the

United States but in the world. He was able to be great and able to be the best at the same time. Do you see what I'm sayin, Tillis? He was a great scorer but he made everyone around him look like a champion, too. His talent brought everyone up to a better level. Kids have to be superior over their peers, they can't be average. It's just not good enough. And if you want to be a professional athlete like you and me, Tillis, it's not always about talent — everybody got talent. It's all about having both physical and mental endurance. It's how long can you go. It's like that in basketball and I KNOW it's gotta be like that in boxing, man. Endurance. If you want it bad enough, you can get it."

# CHAPTER 14

# THINKIN BIG

Imagine you're black. Maybe you are. Imagine you're about six years old, though you're probly not if you're readin this book. Now imagine you are back in the '60s and you get to talk with Cassius Clay, just you and him. When I was six, I imagined that scene. I loved that guy so much I thought he peed ginger ale. I thought maybe he wasn't human. But I imagined somethin that seemed just about impossible for some bad little boy livin in north Tulsa — I imagined talkin to Cassius Clay. I saw it in my head. I believed it enough and wanted it bad enough that it happened. That's what ya gotta do when you think big.

No matter what you want. You wanna be playin basketball for the NBA? Imagine it. You wanna be playin football for the NFL? Imagine it. You wanna be in the White House? Picture yourself sittin in that chair, havin meetins and givin speeches. You might think, "Man, he doesn't know what I'm wantin and where I'm livin. He don't know shit." But I'm tellin you, if you want it bad enough, and if you can see it in your head, you can get there.

But before those pictures get in your mind, you better make sure you got drive. You gotta love what it is that you're after. From the time I first set eyes on Cassius Clay in the Liston fight to the time I saw them signs in my room where my cousin was stayin that said "JAB," "RIGHT CROSS," and

"HOOK," I felt the drive for boxing. It was pullin at my heart and I knew I was in love for good. That's what you gotta feel for the sport you're doin or the job you're wantin. It'll kill ya if you don't love it.

I've talked to a lot of professional athletes, a lot who're in this book — boxers, football players, basketball players, wrestlers — and I respect all sports, but I believe boxing is the most demandin of all. It's because you gotta do it by yourself. You gotta be all man. It's the toughest game there is. I'm tellin you, you take a beatin and it's all on you. You don't get to share your pain with someone else. You gotta sacrifice everythin — important stuff like ice cream, cakes, pies, and makin love.

Some of my brothers and sisters think that if they don't have no money, they ain't worth nothin. They can't get nowhere. But if you got a drive, a love for somethin, the money will come. People will see you workin hard, like they did with me, seein me runnin at 5 AM every mornin before school, runnin to the gym after school to jump rope and throw some combinations, runnin home after practice to get some sleep so I could get up early the next mornin to run again. They'll notice your love and the money will come. It happened to me and I was about as poor as it gets in Tulsa.

Lawrence Lakey had to remind me of this drive one day in the Sea King restaurant.

"I saw Tillis sittin all alone at a table," he remembers. "I was workin as a minister for the Urban League at the time and went over to him, ya know, to see if I could lift his spirits a little. I'd never met him before, just heard of him. After that, I'd run by to see him at home, checkin on him. Two months later I became to Tillis what Bundini Brown was to Muhammad Ali, a shout man in the corner."

Lakey was great. He'd tell me to suck it up. "Baby, it's

resurrection time. The resurRECtion time is COMing now!" He'd handle things for me in the corner, get my ice bags and water bottles for me, watch my opponents, remind me to stick to my plan.

"Nobody has any idea what boxing is like unless they've done it themselves," he says. "The lifestyle of a boxer deserves total respect. The discipline it takes to get up at 5 AM and run, do calisthenics, work with the rope, spar every day, be away from your family. It's a tough way to make a living.

"And then there's the spiritual side . . .

"Boxers have got to have a strong belief in themselves if they're gonna make it. Quick Tillis had that belief. It's seeing beyond the fight, it's faith that sustains them through the doubts, those things that are beyond the bend. Tillis was strong like Holyfield . . . he believed all things. He hoped all things.

"Quick Tillis was what I call an amalgamation — he was a blend of spirit, street life, and walkin in high places. His love for boxing and his motivation made him a product that rose above whatever current state he was in."

I had a lot of those "current states," like Lakey calls 'em. I've been broke, I've been sick, my mind's been troubled, I've been hungry, and I've been in jail. But I always called on the name of Jesus and He got me through it all. The same night I lost to Tim Witherspoon, my lady left me. But not Jesus. He never left me. And I'm not talkin about the prophet Muhammad — he never died for me. I'm talkin about Jesus.

But here's the deal — when you think big, you can't be messin with stuff that God didn't intend for you to be messin with. God didn't intend for cocaine and crack and alcohol and cigarettes and junk food to be goin into your body. He just gave you one body, so don't go fillin it with no junk. Drink juices that are good for you, eat your vegetables like your mama told you, and get away from those people who are messin with their bodies. That's not thinkin big. If you do what all your friends do, you'll be small like them.

If you're poor, you gotta rise above it like I did. But you can't be blamin your mama or daddy. This is what breaks my heart about the kids today — they don't got no respect for their mother or father. When you're poor, ya gotta know that it's the best your parents could have done for you. I guess you could say that it was bein poor that made me drive harder, it was not havin anythin at all that made me want to have more. If I'd had a lot of money, I'd have been real sorry for the way that I'd turned out. Bein poor can give you more drive than rich kids can ever understand.

You think you wanna get high? There's more to life than that. Respect your mama and daddy, if you have them around, and listen to what they tell you, even if you don't like it. Do the best you can in life and keep God first. The Alpha and Omega, the Father, Son, and Holy Ghost.

Stay in school so you can compete in life. Like I say, "You gotta have an education to comPETE. Without it, life ain't too SWEET." Get through high school at least, go to college if you can. Empty yourself in life — but do it in a legitimate way.

I didn't have no bad habits like drinkin, smokin, or doin drugs, like a lot of professional athletes. I tried smokin cigarettes one time and they just gave me a headache. But it was the women that got me in trouble. Don't mess with girls if you're serious about your sport. I messed around too much and got 'em pregnant. Now that I'm older and smarter, I've learned my lesson. Marriage is sacred and you and me shouldn't be messin around with women till we get married. That's the way it's supposed to be.

Another lesson I've learned through my career is that you

gotta have three important people around — a good manager, a good trainer, and a good promoter. I got lucky with my manager and found one who had money and, of course, I can't say enough good about Don King and Bob Arum who were top-notch promoters for me, but the trainer? I got unlucky with him, got taken big time. But still, if you go into professional boxing, remember these three people are the important ones.

You gotta look for the guys who can take you to the top, a trainer who can teach you all the chapters. I learned a few chapters in Tulsa with Ed Duncan, and when I went to Chicago, I learned more of the book — all kinds of combinations like Ray Charles and shoeshinin, more of the basics, and feintin. Learn it all. And if things go wrong, put your head back up and keep goin.

Before I fought Tyson, I had a lot of things goin wrong, me gettin tired and not knowin why. But I heard a big band song one time that was sayin "you gotta have heart, miles and miles of heart." A lot of things will go wrong in life but you gotta have heart. You can't ever give up.

Great athletes come from great athletes, it's the athlete blood runnin through the veins. I got mine from Theodore Hawkins. I passed it on to my first daughter, Iciss Tillis. Maybe you heard of her.

They say she's the best high-school senior in basketball in the nation. The press calls her the "queen of Tulsa girls high school basketball, the city's most highly recruited female player, the best all-around player Oklahoma has ever produced, the number-one-ranked forward among all seniors . . . the most sought-after girl's basketball player in state history." Man.

She got her pick of colleges to go to and she's decided on Duke. I read in the papers that when my baby plays ball, "a coaching convention's worth of people [are there] to watch

[her]." Before she chose Duke, they was all after her — "it will be like winning a lottery to get her to sign a college letter of intent," they said. Like Mama used to say, "I'm prouder of her than a game rooster." Like Archie Moore used to say, "I'm happier than a sissy in a cc camp."

She started out a lot like me, not many people knowin much about her. Then they started to notice the girl with the easy shot, puttin some magic on the ball. She went overseas, playin for the 1998 Team USA at the World Youth Games in Russia — the youngest member on the team — and she's got an automatic bid to try out for the 2000 USA Olympic team. She's got my height and strength, quickness and agility. She's even taller than me. We look great in *Sports Illustrated* together, with her beautiful 6'4" figure standin beside her 6'2" cowboy daddy. She's knockin off my cowboy hat with my boxing gloves on her hands. Real cute picture out in the Oklahoma prairie.

It made me get tears in my eyes when I saw what she said in the newspaper. The words could have come outta my own mouth 20 years ago: "I owe everything to my mom and God," she said. Me too. Mama and God Almighty. Iciss's mama, my Jane Fonda, got her where she is today. Her mama did a good job with her, raisin her while I was on the road fightin, puttin her through school without my help. Iciss has used her ability to go far in school and in basketball.

She'll make it in the pros. I watch her play ball and see myself in her. When she runs the ball down the court or pulls her team ahead, I see that same kinda drive I had. It's a Tillis thing. And though I can't take no credit since I wasn't there for her and her mama, I can still love her and be mighty proud of her. Hey, she's my flesh and blood. I'll always love her.

A lot has changed since my glory days. It was a lotta fun, a lotta hard work, a lotta lessons learned bout trustin people, messin round with women, and gettin back up when others knock ya down.

*You don't float like a butterfly or sting like a bee*
*Because you ain't Ali*
*You the fightin cowboy*
*You ride 'em, rope 'em, brand 'em, corral 'em, and rustle 'em*
*You the fightin cowboy,*
*Old dude.*

That's me, James 'Quick' Tillis, the fightin cowboy who's thinkin big. It's been years since I sat in that jail cell for a month — a month that gave me all the time in the world to think about my story and get it down on paper. The paper's all dried up and yellow now, and I guess it's time to be ridin off into the sunset, waitin for that ranch and sorrel horse to come my way. Yeah, I've paid my dues to the world of boxing and that world has helped me think big. It saved me. It's like what Bundini Brown told me one time, "When a soldier's in battle, you don't show 'im how to shoot a gun. You tell 'im how to take the mountain." That's what thinkin big is all about. You gotta take that mountain, even if it's right in front of you.

## PROFESSIONAL RECORD OF
## JAMES QUICK TILLIS

**BORN**      July 5, 1957

**RECORD**      42 wins; 16 knockouts; 22 losses; 68 total fights

**HEIGHT**      6′2″

**DIVISION**      Heavyweight

**REACH**      78″

**MANAGER**      Don Jackson

**HOMETOWN**      Tulsa, Oklahoma

**TRAINER**      Ronnie Warrior

1999      Washington
Lost in the tenth round to **Tim "The Hebrew Hammer" Hamner**

1998      Oklahoma
Exhibition fight with **"American Native Nightmare" Jason Nickels**

1995      Vancouver
Lost an eighth-round TKO to **Keith Couser**

1995      Vancouver
Won an eighth-round WIN over **Craig "Butterball" Payne**

1995      Colorado
No contest with **Will Hinton**

1993      Ohio
Lost in the tenth round to **Alexander Zolkin**

1993    Illinois
Won a third-round TKO over **"Jack Johnson" Jackson**

1992    Illinois
Won a ten-round WIN over **Danny Blake**

1991    New Jersey
Lost a first-round TKO to **Tommy "Gun" Morrison**

1990    Virginia
Won a third-round TKO over **Carlton West**

1990    Indonesia
Exhibition fight with **Larry Holmes**

1989    Brazil
Lost in the tenth round to **Adilson "Magilla" Rodrigues**

1989    Michigan
Lost in the tenth round to **Arthel Lawhorne**

1988    England
Lost a fifth-round TKO to **Gary Mason**

1988    Nevada
Lost a fifth-round KO to **Evander "Angelo" Holyfield**

1988    England
Lost a fifth-round TKO to **Frank Bruno**

1988    Nevada
Won a second-round TKO over **Rod Smith**

1987    New Jersey
Won a fifth-round TKO over **Dennis Jackson**

1987    South Africa
Lost a tenth-round TKO to **Johnny DuPlooy**

1987    Illinois
Exhibition fight with **Mike "The GOrilla" Tyson**

1987    England
Lost a fifth-round TKO to **Frank Bruno**

1987    Arkansas
Won a fifth-round TKO over **Lorenzo Boyd**

1987    Texas
Lost an eighth-round TKO to **Mike Williams**

1986    Nevada
Draw in the tenth round with **Avery Rawls**

1986    Pennsylvania
Knocked out **Lorenzo Boyd** in the second round

1986    Texas
Won a tenth-round WIN over **Eddie Richardson**

1986    Australia
Lost a tenth-round decision to **Joe Bugner**

1986    Kentucky
Won an eighth-round WIN over **Art Terry**

1986    Oklahoma
Knocked out **Mark Young** in the eighth round

1986    New York
Lost a tenth-round decision to **Mike Tyson**

1986    Pennsylvania
Lost an eighth-round decision to **Tyrell Biggs**

1985    South Africa
Lost a tenth-round decision to **Gerrie "Bionic Right Hand" Coetzee**

1985    Nevada
Lost a tenth-round decision to **Marvis Frazier**

1984    Illinois
Won a tenth-round decision over **Basheer Wadud**

1984    New Jersey
Lost a tenth-round decision to **Carl "The Truth" Williams**

1984    Oklahoma
Knocked out **Michael Bennett** in the first round

1984    Oklahoma
Knocked out **Billy "Fightin Hillbilly" Thomas** in the third round

1984    Oklahoma
Knocked out **Bobby Crabtree** in the third round

1984    Arkansas
Knocked out **Otis Hardy Bates** in the second round

1983    Ohio
Lost a first-round TKO to **"Terrible" Tim Witherspoon**

1983    Illinois
Knocked out **Lynwood Jones** in the fourth round

1983    Illinois
Knocked out **Larry Givens** in the second round

1983    Illinois
Knocked out **Grady Daniels** in the fourth round

1983    Illinois
Won a tenth-round WIN over **Leroy Boone**

1982    Texas
Lost an eighth-round TKO to **Greg Page**

1982    Ohio
Lost a ninth-round TKO to **Pinklon "Pinky" Thomas**

1982    Nevada
Won a tenth-round WIN over **Earnie "The Acorn" Shavers**

1982    Nevada
Knocked out **Jerry Williams** in the third round

1981    Illinois
Lost a fifteen-round decision to **Mike "The Beaver" Weaver**

1981    Illinois
Won a tenth-round WIN over **Tom "Ruffhouse" Fisher**

1980    Illinois
Won a fourth-round TKO over **Domingo D'Elia**

1980    Illinois
Won a tenth-round WIN over **Mike Koranicki**

1980    Illinois
Won a fourth-round TKO over **Eric Sedillo**

1980    Illinois
Won a tenth-round WIN over **Walter Santemore**

1980    Illinois
Won a second-round TKO over **Frank Schram**

1980    Illinois
Won a seventh-round TKO over **Ron Stander**

1980    Illinois
Won a tenth-round WIN over **Dean "Cookie" Wallace**

1979    Oklahoma
Knocked out **Al "Memphis" Jones** in the fourth round

1979    Illinois
Knocked out **Harry Terrell** in the first round

1979    Illinois
Knocked out **Bob Whaley** in the first round

1979    Illinois
Knocked out **Jimmy Cross** in the second round

1979    Illinois
Won a second-round TKO over **Charles Atlas**

1979    Illinois
Won a sixth-round TKO over **Henry Porter**

1979    Illinois
Won a fifth-round TKO over **George Goforth**

1979    Illinois
Knocked out **Rocky Lane** in the first round

1979    Illinois
Won a third-round TKO over **Sylvester Wilder**

1979    Illinois
Knocked out **Dave Watkins** in the second round

1978    Illinois
Won a first-round TKO over **Al Bell**

1978    Illinois
Won a first-round TKO over **Ron Stephany**

# APPENDIX 2

## JAMES 'QUICK' TILLIS' MANAGERS, PROMOTERS, AND TRAINERS

### MANAGERS
Robert Hudson
Jim Kaulentis
Van Eden and Steve Collison
Gary Bentley
"Willy B"
Abe Hurshler
Lenita Tillis
Don Jackson

### PROMOTERS
Ernie Terrell
Bob Arum
Don King
Cedrick Kushner

### TRAINERS
Ed Duncan
DeDe Armour
Rory O'Shea
Shawn Curtain
Archie Moore
Johnny Lira
Harry Wilson
Angelo Dundee
"Willy B"
Drew Bundini Brown
Whit Lawry
Jim Strickland
"Scrap Iron" Johnson
Walter Tyler
Tony "Bossman" Meryll
Johnny Toco